AF434462

It's That Same Story Again - Part 1
by Mark Stroderd

Another 15 Seconds of Life, Bible, and Christian Hebrew

What happens when we recognize the impact of 15-second experiences on the plot of life? Those 15-second experiences could be an abusive and/or blessed homelife, a faithless and/or Christian homelife, wealth and/or poverty, near death experiences and/or miraculous healings, a failed marriage, and/or an angelic wife, broken homes and/or adopted children, and the list continues? Could all of that actually happen within one home? If so, what happens when "that guy" learns how to read Biblical Hebrew and adds 15-seconds to Biblical stories you already know? *It's That Same Story Again* with 15-second experiences that change the plots of Life, Bible, and Christian Hebrew? And the plot begins 15 seconds into the story.

Blessings to all that I have hurt. You are the greatest inspiration that keeps me sharing. Only my God can make things right. This is the story of my travels asking Him to do so. I can only trust that He did and maybe one day you can let me know.

Blessings to all that hurt me. It took me decades to learn what to do when I am hurt. God showed me my role in that pain. Your influence is not small.

Thank you all that love me I couldn't have done this without you.

Thank you, my sweet Lisa. Everyone that knows you knows what I am talking about.

Join me as I share the true story of Life, Bible, and Christian Hebrew.

Psalms 22:1 KJV: *My God, my God, why hast thou forsaken me?*

Table of Contents

Chapter 1

Gal (גל) – Revealed

Life

It's May 6, 2005, and I am awakened by a doctor's voice, "Mr. Stroderd, hello. I am your doctor. What is your wife's name?"

I thought this was only in the movies and it's never good. I replied and she asked if I believed myself capable of understanding her and I replied yes.

Doctor continues, "I have awakened you from a medically induced coma. You are experiencing a brain hemorrhage, and you are feeling no pain because of the morphine. However, if you look to your left, you will see that your heart rate and your blood pressure are extremely high. Your body is only capable of enduring another fifteen minutes. Do you know God?"

I responded with a resounding, "Yes!"

Doctor continues, "Good, I am going to step to the other room, and I will be back in fifteen minutes. If you are alive, we will transport you downtown for emergency surgery tomorrow morning, otherwise we will call the coroner. It is that serious, do you understand?"

I replied, "Hey Doc, nobody is dying today."

The doctor had an encouraging laugh, and everyone leaves me to solitude.

Immediately I knew life would never be the same, *just wasn't aware of how much.*

It was such a simple prayer. I simply looked up and expressed my repentance for making a mess of my life and if He would give me one more chance that I would do my best to make it right. As quickly as those words came out, my body went into complete rest. It literally took less than 15 seconds. Evidently my vitals were visible outside the room because the doctor returned immediately with amazement and had me transported for surgery the following day.

There were eleven of us awaiting surgery due to brain hemorrhaging. The doctor again openly declared that at least seven of us would die that day. He then gave me a phone to call my kids because my scenario was the gravest. I will share that phone call conversation later.

I remember them taking me into surgery. I recall that the room was cold. The next thing I remember was waking up in my room and the doctor visited and explains that while in surgery there was a monitor that provided visual imaging of the blood hemorrhaging into my brain cavity. He continued explaining that minutes before they were to begin surgery the hemorrhaging stopped and that the body has the natural ability to remove the internal bleeding and heal everything.

After he walks out it becomes more real to me that my Creator chose to miraculously heal me while on the operating table. I would share that with every visitor to my room, but I could see it is impossible for anyone to fully comprehend this experience. I am alive, nonetheless, morphine became the priority of the day for the following week. (Month of May Miracle #1)

Seven days later I left the hospital and went to CVS pharmacy to get my prescription filled and the pharmacist asked me what illness I experienced. I replied that I had experienced a subarachnoid brain hemorrhage. He told me that I was prescribed 600 Vicodin pills and voluntarily expressed that I would be in a lot of pain for the remainder of my life. I went home and experienced pain and took my first two pills. Afterwards I was determined to never take another pill. I was healed by God and refused to minimize that miracle to a lifetime addiction of pain pills. I donated the pills to a friend struggling with the pains of cancer. I never felt pain again. (Month of May Miracle #2)

I am recovering rapidly and able to attend my daughter's high school graduation, more than five hours away. I feel feeble but doing my best not to look feeble. She is giving the Valedictorian speech. I am totally aware that my experience at this event is different than everyone else's. My attendance is miraculous, and I know it and it seems nobody else does. Amazing how life stories can become today's news and be forgotten quickly.

Seven days later, May 20th, I returned to work. Everyone was surprised to see me. I am a software engineering consultant and was sent to a company named Million Air where I met their Chief Technology Officer named Bruce. We worked in the same office together and about three days later started sharing our life stories. I shared the 8-hour version of my recent brain hemorrhage story and when done Bruce expressed that he wouldn't believe it until he talked with his wife who is the research nurse at that hospital.

Bruce returned to work the next day, closed the door, and raised his voice louder than the jet engines outside and asked me who the hell I was. He expressed that he is a God serving man and doesn't believe in circumstance and truly wanted to know why God had put us together. He added that his wife, Brenda, said that the hospital wanted me to return for a brain scan and document the healing. I am working with the husband of the research nurse that witnessed and documented my miraculous healing on the operating table. (Month of May Miracle #3)

Life will never be the same.

It's January 2024, and I remember those seven days in the hospital in 2005 very well. Though it was my first life-threatening experience (yes, there is another), it wasn't my first miraculous experience that left me with continually changing answers to the same questions. It took countless experiences and decades of searching before those answers quit changing. And when I finally got the final answer, I realized it was all about the journey. A journey of life, Bible, and Hebrew.

My favorite scripture that led my path on this journey is Proverbs 25:2.

Proverbs 25:2 KJV: It is the glory of God to conceal a thing: but the ***honour of kings*** is to search out a matter.

I was shocked to learn that my God conceals things on purpose. Even more shocked to learn that He takes glory in it. And yet again, He calls my efforts to search out what He has concealed "The Honor of Kings". Exercising my privilege of the *Honor of Kings* and searching out the concealed glory of God continues to this day. Join me as I share my journey of *"The Honor of Kings"* and search out the concealed glory of God.

Christian Hebrew Study

Bob, a former Christian, and now outspoken atheist was talking to Jiff, a Christian brother from his past, *"Let me make sure I understand and don't interrupt. You still believe that if Adam and Eve would not have eaten from the tree, that they would still be alive in the garden. You claim that death is the penalty of sin, so if you don't eat the tree then you have no sin and live forever. But you also believe in a Savior that died that never sinned. You can't have it both ways. If the penalty of sin is death, then how can you claim that your Savior, who died, was without sin? I never understood it. Those two stories contradict each other and it's ridiculous for the churches to think they can have it both ways. You must pick a side, either the penalty of sin is death, or it isn't. How can you explain it?"*

Jiff replies, "*Bob, I love the question. Please don't interrupt because I think I have an answer for you. The Book of Matthew 26:53-54 tells of the situation in the Garden of Gethsemane where Peter cuts off the ear of a man trying to arrest Jesus. Jesus miraculously heals the man's ear then declares to Peter that He could pray to His Father and He would immediately send more than twelve legions of Angels. Then Jesus asked Peter that if He did that then how would the scriptures be fulfilled?*

Jesus didn't die because of any sin committed. He willfully stayed on the cross until His death to fulfill the scriptures. He literally chose not to come off the cross. If He had committed one sin, then He would have justly died on the cross for His own sin. His willingness to stay on the cross, and His choice to accept the penalty of sin, all resulted in His death. His willful <u>death</u> is the sole act of Him becoming sin. His only participation in the sin story is His death, the penalty of sin. His death is synonymous with Him becoming sin."

I share this fictitious story as an example of my ability to join Jiff and see Bob as opposition to my beliefs and faith. What's even more amazing is that I have this unexplainable desire to want Jiff to answer Bob with my own words. I don't disagree with Jiff; I would simply say it differently. There are words that Jiff used that I wouldn't. I want to answer Bob's accusations my own way and though I think Jiff got it right, I would have answered it using different words than Jiff.

Yes, I could continue that thought of critiquing Jiff. There are so many sermons and Bible studies from my past that are at total recall that I could use to answer Bob. Bottom line is that though Jiff answered the question, it is nearly impossible to get 100% approval from all believers of the Gospel with Jiff's choice of words. As fellow believers we reserve the right to answer questions with our own understanding and many times hold our Christian brothers accountable if they use what I call a "reserved word" improperly.

Something as simple as calling new understanding of scripture "knowledge" rather than "revelation" can be a struggle for some Christians. For some, years of study and Church has developed a list of "reserved words". There are moments when I find it difficult to categorize what I learn as knowledge attained from my own efforts or a gift or revelation from my Savior. I will not share my internal battle to simply pick a category and begin writing. I pray you find my use of these words interchangeable and not offensive. For certain I would ask everyone, especially my own kids, to search out what I am sharing for yourself. I am not implying that what I am sharing is something you could only learn from me. Most of what I share has been attained from others and everything I share has been searched out. I am not a prophet or an oracle. I am merely a Christian that has been saved by the Gospel and love my Savior. I can only wish I was as weird as my kids believe me to be. (smile)

I have attended community Bible studies for decades. During that time, I have witnessed more than one hundred English translations published and made available either electronically or at the local Bible Book Store or both. I remember when the Living Bible was published back in the 70's. I recall it not being received well. Now, I often witness Bible Study attendees taking turns sharing their translation of a particular verse because it is different than another in the room. I am thinking this is a common occurrence at group Bible studies.

Any of us could make a visit to the local Bible Book store and select from an assortment of available versions of the Bible. I am **_unaware_** that any of the available versions have been endorsed or opposed by any church. I am unaware of any church organization establishing any form of requirements that a version must meet before it is deemed approved. I might not be 100% correct, but it appears that the only requirement for a version of the Bible to be accepted as the divine and inspired Word of God is for it to have the words "Holy Bible" on the cover. Make your own opinion.

Hello, I am a devout believer that my salvation is in the Gospel of Jesus Christ. I believe He was born of a virgin. I believe, I believe, I believe. Simply check all the boxes. In recent years, sadly after my children were grown and no longer under my care, I decided to learn how to read Hebrew. Like my example of Jiff (above), I can only request your tolerance of my choice of words as I share the simple to understand beauty of the original Hebrew text. I can only pray that one day my kids will read this book while accepting my apology for not knowing until after they left home. Hopefully every parent that reads this will appreciate and find this book something to endorse and share. I am grateful to all that participated and helped. Your input and assistance provided the balance of sharing without an offensive agenda, while at the same time respecting that the story must be told. Thank you!

Thankfully kids, you are all believers. I pray the hard work and tireless research to provide you these stories of Life, Bible, and Hebrew impact your lives and the lives of generations to come. Love me as I do my best to share. Love you.

Honor of Kings

It's January 29, 2024, and after learning and studying Hebrew, I am still lacking wisdom of how to share my newly found understandings. I must learn the right spirit and method of sharing these amazing understandings of my Father's language. It's impossible to exaggerate the disappointment of my failures. Oh Lord, help me get it right this time. Amen

Imagine visiting a Bible study and one of your friends declaring that they have decided to study the Bible one word at a time. Craziness, right? Well, consider that the word "formed" is in the KJV thirty-one times but the Hebrew word U-iitzr (וייצר) translated as "formed" in Genesis 2:7 is a unique Hebrew word only spoken by our Creator one time in the original Hebrew text. I have not confirmed but have been told that there are approximately 31,000 words in the Hebrew text that are only used one time. I have confirmed that there are lots of unique words, I just don't have the ability to count them. Can you think of one English word in the KJV that is used only once in the Bible? Yes, I was determined to find that, and I did! The word "direction" is in the KJV one time. More amazing is that the word "directions" is not in the KJV. Congratulations, you have just completed your first "one word at a time" study of the Bible.

Matthew 4:4 KJV: But he answered and said, It is written, Man shall not live by bread alone, but by every word that proceedeth out of the mouth of God.

Again, I chose to understand what Jesus says in this verse to mean exactly what He says. Join me as we combine what God tells us in Proverbs 25:2 with what Jesus tells us in Matthew 4:4. We will exercise the *Honor of Kings* and search out ONE SINGLE WORD in the original Hebrew text to determine and its use in the English translations to see if it will bring us LIFE. One of my definitions of LIFE is revelation of new understanding that strengthens our faith. To accomplish this, I hope to establish an easy to read and *exciting learning exercise method* as we share many stories of my family's miraculous life events.

Because there are wonderful amounts (LOTS) of research, I chose to give the results of the research which are sometimes followed by pages of documentation (optional reading) to prove the research. Many times, the documentation of the research provides further revelation.

Let's prove that there is life (added revelation) in each word spoken from the mouth of God by exercising the *Honor of Kings* and search out what is concealed in the root Hebrew word for "Reveal" which is Gal (גל). Gal (גל) is found 10 times in the original Hebrew Old Testament called the Tanakh. Let's review how this word is used in those scriptures.

The first five occurrences of the word Gal (גל) are translated in the KJV as HEAP and related to a Heap of Stones.

The next four occurrences of the word Gal (גל) in the KJV it is translated as a verb and refers to something being rolled or removed to expose. Yes, the exact same word is translated as a verb rather than a noun. Yes, the word changes its definition.

The tenth occurrence in the KJV of the word Gal (גל) relates to His darling bride in a private garden.

Combining the revelations of those ten occurrences reveals that the glory of God concealed by the single word Gal is:

Roll away the stone and reveal my Savior has resurrected to create a private garden for His darling bride to share eternity!

Glory to the King!

Isn't that beautiful? The concealed revelation of the word REVEAL in the Old Testament tells us about the resurrection story of our Savior. Wow! Is that life?

Honor of Kings – The Searching Out (optional)

The remainder of this chapter will seem like documentation and education, but again, I prefer to describe it as a privilege and my understanding of *"The Honor of Kings"*. God knows how much joy it was having this revealed and then packaging it for your pleasure. That said, it is the analytical documentation proving the results of the research. Enjoy! May I suggest that you read and enjoy as you would a church service. Do your best not to impose memorizing or learning but rather enjoy it as though you are fellowshipping with the Word (Jesus).

This is our first documentation, and we will only share this information in this paragraph one time. I agree with many and describe the learning of each letter in Hebrew as milk, and each word as meat. In Hebrew, each letter has 1) a definition which provides a depth of meaning, 2) a word (generally three letters) that is enunciated exactly like the letter and adds further clarity of understanding, and 3) a numeric value. The 1st letter of Hebrew is the Alef and the 2nd is the Bet, so when you combine the first two letters of the Hebrew you get the word "Alef Bet" which is where English gets the word Alphabet. There are amazing internet videos that provide a two-hour study on each Hebrew letter. There are 22 letters so in less than 50 hours you can learn the Hebrew AlefBet. It is truly that easy. And, like English, once you know the letters, you can immediately read the language. But what is amazing is that the definition of the Hebrew word is within the combined definition of the letters. The Creator's language is BEYOND GENIUS. Now let's review the meaning of the two Hebrew letters in the spelling of Gal (גל) and the concealed revelations of this word.

Gal Wave(?) גל

One of the internet search engines translates Gal being the word wave. I often utilize various search engines to get a quick translation of a particular word from English to Hebrew or visa-versa. I realize that the information provided from a search engine is nothing more or less than another translator using technology to provide yet another translation. Today, one of these search engines openly declares that it accesses the latest AI (Artificial Intelligence) tools which again, is nothing but another translation. I struggle forcing the interpretation to be Wave. Well, thank you God for your heavenly language which provides us the definition of a word by researching the definition of the letters that spell the Word. Yes, Hebrew sounds like a difficult language but as we continue, you will see that it is truly a language of the heart and requires minimal cerebral assistance.

Hebrew is read right to left so the first letter of the word Gal (גל) is Gimel (ג) which means Camel or Wealth. The last letter is the Lamed (ל) which means Authority or Shepherd's hook.

The Hebrew letters that spell the word Gal (גל) define it as
The Wealth (ג) of Authority (ל)

Oh my! Can I explain this with clarity? There is no wealth more valuable than the wealth of God. He ordained a letter within His language to assist us to understand that. That letter Gimel (ג) represents a Camel or Great Wealth. I think the letter looks like a camel. Remember Abraham sent his unnamed faithful servant with ten camels of wealth and his son to go find his son a bride. Those camels carried some of Abraham's wealth. Is it surprising that we are learning that His wealth is concealed in His revelations. Later we will search out other Hebrew letters that further reveal that understanding. Only God has the authority to reveal His wealth.

So hopefully now you can appreciate that I have chosen to research the variations of the word "reveal" that are used in scripture. Let's see if we can search out some of His wealth. Enjoy the journey and prepare for an amazing revelation as we reveal the revelations of the Hebrew words translated as "reveal", "revealeth" and "revealed" in the KJV translation of the divine and inspired Word of God.

The word **"revealed"** is found in the Old Testament of the KJV 13 times. There are nine different Hebrew words translated as "revealed". Those nine Hebrew words are in the Hebrew Old Testament (called Tanakh) 27 times. Below are the nine Hebrew words and how many times each Hebrew word is found in the Hebrew Old Testament (Tanakh). When the word is found one time, then the verse is also provided. Note that the common letters found in each word are (**גל**) and have a bold font.

והנגלת One time (Deuteronomy 29:29)

יגלה Seven times

נגלה Four times

גליתה One time (2 Samuel 7:27)

ונגלה Six times

נגלתה One time (Isaiah 53:1)

להגלות One time (Isaiah 56:1)

גליתי Three times

גלי Three times

Likewise, below are the three Hebrew words that were translated as **"reveal"** in the KJV. These three Hebrew words are found in the Tanakh 9 times.

יגלו Three time

וגליתי Five times

למגלא One time (Daniel 2:47)

One more time, below are the five Hebrew words translated as **"revealeth"**. These five Hebrew words are in the Tanakh 44 times.

מגלה Nine times

גלה Twenty-Three times

גולה Nine times -- eight of nine refer to deportation of some sort

גלא Two times (Daniel 2:22, 2:28 revealer of secrets)

וגלא One Time (Daniel 2:29 revealer of secrets)

Summarizing, there are a total of 17 different Hebrew words that are translated as either "Reveal", "Revealeth" or "Revealed" and six of them are unique, only used one time in scripture. These 17 Hebrew words are found in the Hebrew Old Testament (Tanakh) 79 times. These three forms of the word reveal are in the KJV 51 times which means that there are 28 times that these same Hebrew words are translated as something other than these three words in the KJV. All but one of these seventeen Hebrew words contains the word Gal (גל) within their spelling.

To eliminate even the slightest amount of conjecture, let's review the ten verses where the Hebrew word Gal (גל) is used within the Old Testament.

Genesis 31:46 is the first time that both words Gal (גל) and Stones אבנים are in the Hebrew text. Note that the first time the word "stones" is in the KJV is Genesis 28:11 and it is not the same Hebrew word nor the same spelling.

Genesis 31:46 KJV: And Jacob said unto his brethren, Gather stones (אבנים); and they *took stones* (אבנים), *and made an heap* (גל)[1]: and they did eat there upon the heap (הגל)[0].

Note that in verse 45 that Jacob (Israel) erects a stone as a pillar (monument). Now his brethren Gather stones and make a *heap (mound) of stones*, and they eat. Also notice that the last word heap in Genesis 31:46 is not the root word spelling of reveal, so it has a superscript value of zero.

Joshua 7:26 KJV: Then they raised over him *a great heap* (גל)[2] *of stones* (אבנים), still there to this day. So the Lord turned from the fierceness of His anger. Therefore the name of that place has been called the Valley of Achor to this day

Joshua 8:29 KJV: And the king of **Ai** (העי) he hanged on a tree until evening. And as soon as the sun was down, Joshua commanded that they should take his corpse down from the tree, cast it at the entrance of the gate of the city, and raise over it *a great heap* (גל)[3] *of stones* (אבנים) that remains to this day.

Hilarious, the King of (AI – artificial intelligence) is hanged from a tree.

2 Samuel 18:17 KJV: And they took Absalom and cast him into a large pit in the woods, and laid *a very large heap* (גל)[4] *of stones* (אבנים) over him. Then all Israel fled, everyone to his tent.

Job 8:17 KJV: His roots are wrapped *about the heap* (גל)[5], and seeth the place of *stones* (אבנים).

So, the first five occurrences of the word Gal (גל) it is translated as HEAP and related to a Heap of Stones. Let's continue.

> **Psalms 22:8** KJV: He ***trusted*** (גל)[6] ***on the LORD*** (יהוה) that he would deliver him: let him deliver him, seeing he delighted in him.

Note that several translations (NASB 1995, Living Bible, etc.) translate this as literally meaning To Roll to the LORD.

> **Psalms 119:18** KJV: ***Open thou*** (גל)[7] mine eyes, that I may behold wondrous things out of thy law.

Also translated as "Expose or Reveal Yourself" to my eyes.

> **Psalms 119:22** KJV: Remove (גל)[8] from me reproach and contempt; for I have kept thy testimonies.

> **Proverbs 16:3** KJV: Commit (גל)[9] thy works unto the LORD (יהוה), and thy thoughts shall be established.

Again, other translations (NASB 1995, Legacy Standard Bible, etc.) translate this as literally meaning To Roll thy works unto the LORD.

So, the previous four verses show the occurrences of something being rolled or something done to expose something. Now it's time to see His wealth, the "thing" He chose to conceal and requires me to search out. The last occurrence of Gal is located in the book of the Song of Solomon. Hilarious, right? A book so difficult to understand and seldom researched. What a GREAT PLACE to conceal something!

> **Song of Solomon 4:12** KJV: "My ***darling bride is like a private garden*** (גל)[10], a spring that no one else can have, a fountain of my own.

The final, tenth occurrence of the word is translated as a private garden in the King James and is compared to "My darling bride". I cannot find words to bring more understanding to what the verse reads.

Glory to the King!

Chapter 2

Gilgal (גלגל) – To Roll

Life

I don't recall the date of my first visit to Bruce's home, but I do remember it was an awesome visit. His daughter had already grown up and moved out and his two sons were freshmen in high school. It had to be July or August of 2005 because we all enjoyed watching the boys play on the JV football team. They are freshmen, but they are so athletic that they are playing 10th grade football. In Texas, that is everything! Sure, I recall the first visit went well and that is awesome because when football season started, the fun began.

What a family. Brenda, the research nurse, literally put this family together. No kidding. The kids are all adopted, and it only takes a couple visits to know that the spirit of this home was influenced by mom. The story of the adoption of each of these kids is crazy beautiful. So beautiful and personal that they should only be told by the family. How this family came together is nothing short of miraculous and it begins with Bruce experiencing a near death experience. Sound familiar?

Like most successful marriages, Bruce just didn't deserve a wife like Brenda. When I first got to know her, she immediately became my best understanding of a saint. She is a blonde, petite and full of energy. Anyone that shows up will have to turn down food. No, I don't mean because she asks, I mean because she is bringing you a plate and you literally will have to say no, which I never did.

When moms are good cooks, the boys become football beasts. The first kid they adopted was James, but he is also the youngest. Hilarious, right? Most families' first child is their oldest. I have never witnessed such a good-natured old soul of a kid. But, when he puts on a football helmet, he will absolutely reset your clock. The boy has brute strength and has never heard the word fear.

The second child they adopted was Jacob. Jake is the opposite body style of his brother. He is slightly taller but wiry. He isn't scared of anything and is equally fierce on the football field. He and his brother both play defensive end, and it is a show worthy of the cost of a ticket to watch these two boys. Man, I am having so much fun! Did I mention we watched a lot of football games?

Many years later I would meet their third adopted kid named Brittany. Like all the kids, she is as unique as they come.

It's really simple. Someone other than me could produce a movie series on this family, but only because of Brenda. I can assure you that everyone that knows this family would agree that the movie would have been named Brenda. Bruce, the kids, the church, the high school, the waitresses at the restaurants, and everybody else that knows these guys would agree with me. It's all about Brenda.

Love you Brenda!

Christian Hebrew Study

It's August 2020 and Lisa and I have been trying to find a new home. For three months now we have been parking our RV in towns further from where we currently live to find the place that we will recognize when we see it. Sherry, Bruce's sister, tells us to come visit Medina, Tx and park our RV at the same park where they live, Farm Country on Ranch Road 2828.

After the move, Lisa goes back home to Alvin while I continue working from home in Medina for a few days. A couple days later, my 1st Saturday in Medina, it's time to discover if this is the place. I drive into the metropolis that doesn't even have a yellow flashing street sign and I see very few places of business. But there is this one place with huge letters at the roof line that says, "Espresso Pizza and Prayer". I love small-town Texas.

I pull in and walk inside to get a cup of coffee. Within a few seconds I realize that the place is closed. Wait a minute, the door is unlocked, and this place is obviously making a Bible Statement but there isn't anyone here. I simply took-in a deep breath and realized *this was the place*. I even noticed that they posted their WiFi password on the napkin holders. This place is beyond cool!

Medina is geographically near the center of the Texas Hill Country which is arguably some of the most beautiful land in Texas. I was told the zip code had 1,744 people but it would seem like much less.

It's Monday, I return to the Espresso Pizza and Prayer place with my computer because the RV Park has poor WiFi and I have work to do. I find a seat and begin my work and now it's time for me to begin my usual "wear out your welcome" routine. It's just my nature to test boundaries. I promise, if God ever sends me to another Medina, I will practice my recluse behavior (if that is possible).

After sharing my Medina stories with Lisa, she returns the following weekend, and we are looking for a place to live in Medina. We visited this RV Park named Rocky Point Retreat and they showed us a small two-story cedar cabin located on the side of the RV Park and has amazing curb appeal. We inspected it and decided it was too small and continued our search. With no success we returned home to Alvin and after further discussion we decided we would try out life in that Medina cabin, and we signed a five-year lease. We live in Medina, the heart of the Texas Hill Country. Wow! What a change.

The stories of Lisa and my first year in Medina deserve far more detail than I will share. The people we met are the most amazing group of people. It would take books and a mini movie series to share the heritage, personalities, and entrepreneurial efforts over several generations required for a place like this to exist and become available for underserving migrants like me. Lisa has joined the garden club, we are attending the local Community Church that has a methodist sign, I have joined the volunteer fire department, assisting residents of our RV community, and I have been privileged to speak many times at that Espresso Pizza and Prayer place.

To further condense that first year, I will add that though Lisa and I have far less to contribute to the community than those who established it, we did give all we had. We gave our time, money, and heart. I'm not saying any of those were requested or required. We gave voluntarily like everybody else does. This town is packed with people that volunteer on a weekly basis. Voluntary participation is something this town schedules which questions the definition of voluntary and muddies the waters of how to work with volunteers. Nonetheless, Lisa and I are part of that schedule. We love Medina.

One year after living in Medina, sixteen years after the brain hemorrhage and *many* miracles later, it's September 19, 2021. A friend called me and expressed that he had attended a Bible study and the people at that study were weird like me. We both laughed as he told me more details, so I attended their next study. I remember the date because it was my daughter's birthday and my friend Les's as well. The Bible study started at 10:00am that morning and within a few minutes I realized that several people study Hebrew. I listened as long as possible before my dominant, obnoxious, passionate, caring, loving, kind, interruptive personality kicked in. I don't know how all those traits were packaged into one body, but here I am, just a messed-up bundle of "wanting to know". I didn't attend with the intention of being disruptive but by the end of that lesson I was far worse than disruptive.

I've been attending church and studying scriptures for four decades. My life story is a mess, but truth be known my life started from a place far from Biblical values and by now I was aware that I only had one life to take this journey to learn and live the truth. During this journey I learned that my passion to know the truth has controlled my existence.

Well, I just couldn't stay quiet. I realized that they were referring to Jesus by the name Yeshua. I was already familiar with Jesus's Hebrew name, so it wasn't something that was going to make me leave the study. Finally, after asking enough questions and already that day's greatest spectacle, I asked the obvious question, "Ok, so every time I ask a question about Jesus, you guys' answer using his Hebrew name. Is there a problem with using Jesus as my Savior's name?"

James was the name of the man leading the study. His reply and the spirit of his reply rocked my world. James simply expressed that over the centuries we truly have lost how to properly enunciate our Savior's name correctly, so since we don't know how to say it, then truly almost any way we have learned it expressed is acceptable. His answer was direct with humility.

James had no idea what was happening to me internally, but he would soon find out. I am convinced that God sent James, a man with a spirit of absoluteness and able to share understanding of the simplest knowledge that had been hidden from me. The knowledge that not only does my Savior bring salvation, but His name is literally Salvation. I cannot express or exaggerate what happened to me in that exact moment, but I know that I received a new understanding.

I went home and began my efforts to learn Hebrew. My sweet wife Lisa witnessed my change of spirit and that once again here goes "Mr. I Have a New Passion". She is so understanding of me. To know me is to know that only Lisa could live with such a man. Lisa watched while I learned how to read Hebrew in 45 days. My friend James and many others at the Bible study considered that miraculous but I struggle giving it that description. It doesn't take a miracle to learn Hebrew. In fact, I believe I am an expert teacher of how to learn it. It's simple. Hebrew is a HEART language and not a BRAIN language.

1 Corinthians 1:27 KJV: But God (יהוה) hath chosen the foolish things of the world to confound the wise; and God (יהוה) hath chosen the weak things of the world to confound the things which are mighty;

One of my personal greatest accomplishments is the ability to put my brain in my pocket and learn Hebrew with my heart. Lisa watched and witnessed moments when I cried from new depth of understanding and moments of disappointment of translation. I am experiencing many joyful moments of revelation like that moment experienced during my first Bible study with people that can read Hebrew. I also experienced many moments where I was utterly irritated at the English words chosen by the various translations.

Honor of Kings

As I attempt to reveal more about the Master's Word Gal (גל) from the previous chapter, I remember in my late 20's that my wife and I visited what I would call a very proper elderly lady. There was just an elegance, an innocence, a beauty of spirit about everything she did and spoke. As we sat on her backyard patio you could see every square inch of the yard was perfectly landscaped and manicured. It was a first-time experience to meet someone of this character and share a moment of innocence. That moment on her back porch was *a revealing* experience. It's what came to mind after my new understanding of Gilgal (גלגל).

Upon initial appearance it is obvious that Gilgal (גלגל) is spelled like Gal (גל) is repeated. Just like when Jesus says, "Verily, verily", Gilgal (גלגל) repeats the spelling of Gal (גל). Gilgal is a verb and in Hebrew it means to roll away. Yes, the place named Gilgal in scripture is like naming a town with a verb like Running. Welcome to Running, Tx. Enjoy as we exercise our privilege of the *Honor of Kings* and search out the meaning of the verb Gilgal.

Everyone that knows me will struggle believing this is my writing. I am far from a poet, but committed to sharing what has been Gal (גל) to me about Gilgal (גלגל). Unlike Gal (גל), the understanding of Gilgal (גלגל) literally flows like sitting on a patio in a well-manicured backyard. So, relax, no memorizing! (laughing)

My version of the definition of the letters that spell Gilgal is, One Revelation (גל) Reveals Another Revelation (גל). Another version of that would be, "The wealth (ג) of authority (ל) leads to more wealth (ג) of authority (ל)." Consider your understanding of Gal (גל) and now convert that to a verb. A revealing is something you see, it's a noun. Gilgal is something you do so that you can see a revealing. Gilgal is like the act of unwrapping a present. Understanding that a present can only be unwrapped once is why there is only ONE GILGAL.

The Same Story Again The Hebrew root word for Gilgal is only used twice in the Old Testament, but variations of the word Gilgal is in our KJV 39 times, and **SUPPOSEDLY** it is not used in the New Testament. Don't get mad! They simply used its definition rather than the word, which we will reveal was a **PERFECT TRANSLATION**. Remember, you can only roll-away something once! Then you give it a name and talk about it. Since there was already a "rolling away" in the Old Testament and it was named Gilgal which means to roll away, the rolling away of the stone to reveal the tomb was empty is a ***New Present*** with a new name. We call it *The Resurrection or First Fruits*, it's not the same unwrapping as *Gilgal*.

Did you know that "First Fruits" is concealed in the first word God ever spoke? We will search that out later.

The story of Gilgal is in Joshua Chapters 4-5. Gilgal is the name given to the place on the other side of the Jordan River where Israel crossed from the wilderness. Just like the Red Sea, the waters of the Jordan were parted, and the people crossed on dry land. Now let's review Joshua 5:9 and the significance of Gilgal.

Joshua 5:9 KJV: And the Lord (יהוה) said unto Joshua, This day have I rolled away (גלותי) the reproach (את- חרפת) of Egypt from off you. Wherefore the name of the place is called Gilgal (גלגל) unto this day.

For me to understand the significance of Gilgal required me to undertake the near impossible exercise of forgetting my past understanding. The most difficult part of my past teaching on Gilgal is the fact that it just wasn't a memorialized story. It never made my top-ten list. Let's fix that.

Below is a list of a few things from Gilgal story. Seeing the events of the story might remind you of a similar New Testament story.

- Joshua 4:19 tells us that this is where they entered the promised land.
- Joshua 4 tells us that the waters of the river Jordan were parted, and they crossed on dry land just like when they left Egypt. Since Egypt

- represents the World, it's as though the waters are like a chasm between God's people and the World.
- The Hebrew word for God Rolled Away is only used one time in scripture.
- This Hebrew word for reproach is in the Old Testament sixteen times and this is the only instance that has the prefix "את" which is the stamp of "The First and The Last", our Savior. We will search out "את" later.
- God rolled away the reproach of Egypt (The World) after they crossed Jordan.
- God rolled away the reproach of Rome (The World) at the tomb.
- Joshua 4:19 tell us they entered the Promised Land on the 10th Day of the 1st Month which is the same date of the Triumphal Entry of Jesus into Jerusalem.
- Joshua 5:9 tells us that at Gilgal God rolled away the reproach (filth) of Egypt from off His people.

The Roman Empire's role in the crucifixion resembles the role of Egypt during the Exodus. Rome judged, sentenced, and crucified Jesus. Then they placed guards to ensure the stone that covered the exit of the tomb would not be rolled away. Just like when Joshua led Israel into the promised land and God rolled away the reproach of Egypt at Gilgal, He also rolled the stone at Jesus's tomb revealing that He was no longer under the reproach of Rome. The story of Gilgal is the concealed Old Testament shadow of the resurrection.

Deuteronomy 11:30 KJV: Are they not on the other side Jordan, by the way where the sun goeth down, in the land of the Canaanites, which dwell in the champaign over against Gilgal (הגלגל), beside the plains of Moreh (מרה)?

The first mentioning of Gilgal is Deuteronomy 11:30 where Moses prophesies in that chapter about the crossing of Jordan. There is so much to unpackage in this verse. Over the next few chapters, we will do the *Honor of Kings* and search out the word Moreh but here is a preview. The definition of the Hebrew letters that spell Moreh is, "The Womb (מ) of the Prince (ר) Revealed (ה)".

At Moreh the waters were bitter, so Moses "flung" a tree (עץ) into the waters, and they became sweet. We will also do the *Honor of Kings* and search out the word Tree but here is a preview. The definition of the Hebrew letters that spell tree (עץ) is, "See (ע) Righteousness (ץ)."

So, in Moreh, Moses flung something visibly righteous into the bitter waters and they became sweet, and the people lived.

Revelation 6:14 KJV: And the heaven departed as a scroll when it is rolled together; and every mountain and island were moved out of their places.

Revelation 6:14 provides another moment where something is "rolled back". When the roll back (Gilgal) happens this time, it will be at His second coming. Could each instance of the letters that spell reveal (Gal גל) in the word Gilgal (גלגל) possibly be related to the revealing of the 1ˢᵗ and 2ⁿᵈ coming where something is rolled back? The first time was a stone, and the second time was the heavens.

We have an amazing journey of revelations to search out. Continue while praying as we roll back (גלגל) to witness what's revealed (גל). I pray the Authority (ל) of Wealth (ג) pours out His riches.

The Hebrew spelling of twenty-three of the thirty-nine occurrences of Gilgal is הגלגל. This is the same spelling used in Deuteronomy 11:30 which has the Hebrew letter Hey (ה) preceding it. When this letter is before a noun it is translated as the word "The". Yes, pretty unremarkable. I have confirmed this "*unremarkableness*" with my Hebrew scholar friends and they have confirmed that it is exactly that, it is simply the word "The". As you can tell, I have a problem with this. This letter is the Revelation letter of Hebrew. It literally means revelation or behold. The pictograph paleo-Hebrew of this letter is a man with his arms raised and likely jumping up and down from excitement. That's more like it! Behold, God has rolled the stone away. Behold, God has rolled away the reproach of Egypt from you. Behold, your Savior has risen. I like BEHOLD! Gilgal (הגלגל) - Behold (ה), One Revelation (גל) Reveals Another Revelation (גל).

Glory to the King!

Chapter 3

Otz (עץ) – Tree, Arz (ארז) – Cedar,
u qutz (וקוץ) – Thorn, and u drdr (ודרדר) – Weed/Thistle

Life

It's only been a few months and already I cannot count the number of times Bruce has been misunderstood by every human on the earth. I'm not kidding! In fact, I have never met a man more misunderstood. It took me a long time to figure out why. I can't say the exact day that it happened, but it took a long time to figure it out. While camouflaging exhaustive efforts to help heal his new co-worker, he could not pretend to be anyone but himself.

It was September 2005, only four months after I began working with Bruce and before the program was implemented. I remember well that it was a Friday. My friendship with Bruce is becoming more like a brother relationship each week. Today, it is the day that Million Air is going to make me an offer of employment. There have been numerous uncommon stories that have occurred in the past four months but today is a big day. Little did I know we would be making jokes about this day for the rest of our career and lives. Remember, I had been working as a contractor since May 20th, just 14 days after my brain hemorrhage. This isn't going to be your ordinary call from the job placement firm to let you know that you got the job.

Bruce plans for us to visit a restaurant, and while there he wrote my salary offer on a napkin. He then tells me that after working with the company for a year and proving that I am trustworthy, then they will increase my compensation.

Bruce and I both have short fuses but his is shorter than mine. I went from excited to hear about the offer to ready to ignite into rage when my character was questioned. I have already worked since May 20th and took very few days off during that stretch. I recall Bruce coming to the office one day telling me that I had to go home. I asked why and he expressed that I had not left the office in three days, and I stink. I was drinking lots of coffee while sitting at a computer and typing code for more than 16 hours on many days. We both laughed. That's just one example that should have satisfied any questions of my character. Now you can see why I was very upset. No, I was insulted and 100% angry (to say it nicely).

I accepted the offer and we returned to the office. Bruce knows I am mad but unlike any other time, he does nothing about it. I finally couldn't take

23

it, so I got up from my desk and went to the office door which was shut. Bruce was sitting with his back to the door and we both knew this was a big moment. When I grabbed the doorknob, without turning his chair, Bruce asked me, "What are you going do?" Somehow, I don't remember him having a loud voice.

This is the 1st big moment of my career with Million Air. Am I going to go back to my chair and just take the insult and prove it wrong? I stood holding the doorknob for at least 15 seconds, seemed like an hour. Bruce never turned to look. It was a quiet standoff. He wasn't typing, and nobody was talking. With humility and embarrassment, I let go of the doorknob and sat back in my chair where when facing my computer, my back faces Bruce's desk.

That story never died and was retold in my presence many times. Regardless of my successes in years to come, the sting of the story never got easier. It's a sting that nobody cares to relive, nor do they care to hear it retold in their presence. Nonetheless, I was able to deal with the fact that I should have never grabbed that doorknob. Now I am an employee of Million Air.

Christian Hebrew Study

It was October 2021 and my wife Lisa, and I live in Medina, Texas. If you are lucky enough to live in Medina, then you are lucky enough. The Texas Hill Country is the place to live. Lisa and I moved here in August 2020 and will likely get buried boots-up in the Hill Country. This place is paradise. We are leasing a little cabin on the side of a hill. It's really easy to find us, just stop anywhere in town and ask where somebody lives. Everybody knows where everybody lives, especially that new outspoken migrant that just showed up from Alvin. (smile)

I was invited for about the seventh time to speak at the local Wednesday evening community Bible study. Being invited to speak on Wednesday's is a privilege. For the first time I have included some of my newly found revelations from my recent Hebrew research. Did you forget who I am? I am older but I am still that dominant, obnoxious, passionate, caring, loving, kind, interruptive person I have always been. Well, add naïve to that list. How could anybody not love what I was learning? Yes, I am THAT STUPID. I would later learn that some people will only tolerate a limited amount OF ME.

Well, one of the elder members of the local community church that enjoys my talks on Wednesdays asked me if I want to lead the adult Sunday School class at the Community Church that we were both attending. I believe he and his wife were founding members from many decades ago. Of course, I see this as God's hand of blessings and accept. It undoubtedly was the blessings of God, but I just wish He would have blessed me with more wisdom than passion. Lord, don't reduce my passion, simply increase my wisdom. (laughing) I am old now and ready to be wise and not pay the price for being over-passionate. I truly mean no harm to anyone.

We met with the Pastor and agreed that I would start teaching the class at the beginning of the year (2022). I decided to visit the class the last weekend of December and learned there were six people attending. During the week I convinced the pastor to allow us to meet in the fellowship hall which wasn't being used. That first weekend of January we had more than ten and I am thankful because I learned that I needed practice and I had not considered making a PowerPoint presentation to both display the topic as well as assist me staying on course. The following weekend we had nearly thirty attending. Though I was still a novice in Hebrew research, I included introductory understandings. I am so grateful for the opportunity to share. The 1ˢᵗ class was on Noah. A Noah lesson like nothing seen before. We will search out Noah in a later book. Noah's name translates to Rest. His two-letter Hebrew name spelled backward is Grace. Hmm. Noah found Grace.

Honor of Kings

Like most common Bible stories, the garden of Eden has points of interest that are almost never shared in a Church or Biblical Study session. One of those points of interest is focused on the fact that the land was cursed because of man's sin. The land didn't do anything wrong. The trees did not sin, yet they were cursed along with the land.

The Hebrew word for tree is Otz (עץ), and it is spelled (from right to left) Ayin (ע), which means eye, and Tsadi (ץ) which means righteousness. The definition of the word derived from the Hebrew letters that spell the word is, "See Righteosness". From the day that I learned this, stepping outside was different.

Romans 8:22 KJV: For we know that the whole creation groaneth and travaileth in pain together until now.

Romans 8:22 tells us that the whole creation groans and travails. I am convinced it's because it is waiting for the curse to be removed. I could be wrong, but I understand "the whole creation" to be everything that lives other than humans. If that is correct, then it is implying that all living things

communicate in some manner with the Creator. I can't explain it but that is
what it seems. I'm not going to *get tangled around the axel* and neither will *I
die on this hill*; (laughing) it's just how I see it.

At the time of this book, I have been studying Hebrew words for nearly
three years. Having attended college, I believe my interest, dedication, and
continued investment to study is beyond the requirements of any college student
that has graduated in the study of Biblical Hebrew. That is not a declaration to
reveal my confessed issues with arrogance, but rather to express how
disappointing it was that I lived nearly the entire allotted time to live before
being introduced to this beautiful language. I won't so badly to blame that on
somebody other than me. He knows that I love His language. Now that I know,
is loving His language in any way related to loving His Word or Words? I don't
know, but I do know that studying Hebrew isn't a burden but rather a privilege.

Very few, almost none, of the proper nouns of the Bible were translated
from the original Hebrew, rather they were transliterated. However, nearly all
the common nouns were translated. I can't make sense of that. Surely by now,
you have used your computer and checked on my understanding of these
Hebrew words. I remember the 1st time I checked these "internet talking heads"
that we call teaching videos. I was far beyond amazement to find that they were
telling the truth. I had no idea that Ruth's name in Hebrew translated to English
as Friend. Or, that Caleb's name in Hebrew as Dog. Or, that Joshua's father's
name Nun means Life. I remember one talking head using humor about Caleb's
loyalty and that his name means dog saying, "Joshua, the son of Life, and his
loyal Dog took the people into the promised land." Yes, that one is humorous
but soon you will see that understanding the translation of these nouns adds
incredible revelation of God's word that would otherwise never be known.

Because most of the common nouns were translated, the names of
many trees are included in scripture. Now that we know that a tree (עץ) means
"See (ע) Righteousness (ץ)", I can only hope we share the anxiety to search out
the spelling of types of trees. That said, we will only search out Cedar (ארז).

The Hebrew word for Cedar is Arz and is spelled ארז. The first letter of
the word is Alef (א) which is the God letter. The second letter is Resh (ר) which
means Prince or Head. The last letter is Zayin (ז) which means Perfection of
Sword. The Zayin (ז) looks very similar to the Vav (ו). The definition of the
Word derived from the letters is, "The Father (God א) and His Son (ר) are
Perfect (ז)."

The Same Story Again And then there was silence! Imagine if the greatest story ever told included providing us with the understanding that trees are a visual image of righteousness and that the Hebrew word for Cedar translates into English as "The Father and His Son are Perfect" or "The Father and the Son are a Sword". Ok, I admit it, telling anyone that Jesus was nailed to a cedar tree is conjecture. That said, I would bet the farm that He was. I believe that similar to the blood of Adam crying out from the ground, that if that uprooted and sawed Cedar Tree could talk, it would say, "He is righteous and perfect!" I would buy another ticket to *The Same Story Told Again* just to see the 15 seconds when that cedar cross screamed.

Let's continue this study by searching out the Hebrew words for Thorn and Thistle. First, we will reveal that the original Hebrew of thorns and thistles in Genesis 3:18 are singular and not plural. Then we will review the revelation from that understanding.

Genesis 3:18 KJV: Thorns (וקוץ) also and thistles (ודרדר) shall it bring forth to thee; and thou shalt eat the herb of the field.

In Hebrew, all plural forms of a noun have the Hebrew letters Yod and Mem (ים) at the end of the noun. Research for yourself and confirm that Genesis 3:18 refers to a single thorn and a single thistle. Also, the first letter of וקוץ is the Vav (ו) and it is translated as the word "And" not provided in the English. The Hebrew word for Thistle is (קוץ).

Now we will review two verses that use thorns and thistles. One provides the plural forms and the other the singular.

In Psalms 118:12 is the example of the plural and Hosea 10:8 is the singular form of these two words.

Psalms 118:12 KJV: They compassed me about like bees: they are quenched as the fire of thorns (קוצים): for in the name of the LORD I will destroy them.

One of the three times that the plural form of thorns is in scripture is in Psalms 118:12. The reason the plural form (קוצים) is not similar to the singular form (קוץ) is because the Hebrew letter Tsadi (צ) is one of five Hebrew letters that is written differently when it is the last letter of the word. So, ץ and צ are the same letter.

Hosea 10:8 KJV: The high places also of Aven, the sin of Israel, shall be destroyed: the thorn (קוץ) and the thistle (ודרדר) shall come up on their altars; and they shall say to the mountains, Cover us; and to the hills, Fall on us.

This verse uses the same form of the words for thorn and thistle as Genesis 3:18 and it translate both words as singular.

__The Same Story Again__ The impact of Genesis 3:18 being singular rather than plural is astounding! First, let's consider a few questions. Do you think Adam knew that the thorn and the thistle were singular instead of plural? Do you think Moses who wrote these words knew he was writing the singular instead of the plural? What changes in the story of Genesis Chapter 3 if the thorn and thistle are singular rather than plural?

Surely, the patriarchs of old knew the thorn and thistle in Genesis 3:18 were singular. Surely, Moses knew it when he scribed it. The big question is, what does that reveal, and did they know?

For all my life I have been correctly taught that the seed of the woman in Genesis 3:15 is prophecy concerning the 1st coming of Jesus. Without providing additional evidence it would be fairly easy to agree that Hosea 10:8 is referring to Jesus's second coming. If Genesis 3:18 is singular, then is it reasonable to consider that this single thorn and single thistle is the same referenced in Hosea 10:8? If so, do the judgments of fall of man in Genesis 3 include prophecy of both the 1st and 2nd coming? Knowing that Genesis 3:18 references the 2nd coming of Christ is equally as priceless as knowing Genesis 3:15 references His first coming. Do you believe the patriarchs of old knew and believed this revelation?

The definition of the words Thorn and Thistle according to the letters that spell them is equally amazing. For thorns (וקרץ) the definition is, "The Straight up Man with the Nail (ו) is Holy (ק), and the Straight up Man with the Nail (ו) is Righteous (ק)." What makes that interesting is to understand that there are people in scripture that are Holy but not Righteous. The definition of the letters for Thistles (ודרדר) is, "The Straight up Man with the Nail (ו) is the Door (ד) to the Prince (ר) is the Door (ד) to the Prince(ר)." Yes, another example of the letters within a word repeating. What's more interesting is that the root word letters (דר) are translated seven times as the word generations. So, Thistles could mean that Jesus is the Door to the Prince (the Resurrected Son of God) for generation after generation.

Glory to the King!

Chapter 4

Chmor (חמור) – Donkey

Life

It was November 2005, and I had been working on this program for nearly six months. The CEO planned a business trip and there are four of us on the private plane, including me and Bruce. On the return we had to stop in Cincinnati to refuel so we also ordered catering for dinner. While at the table there was nothing less than what seemed like a predatorial attack by the CEO towards me because the program wasn't yet in service. In the middle of his attack, Bruce speaks and draws the CEO's attention to himself. Did I mention that Bruce had a loud voice? The insults continue about my efforts, but nobody is looking at me, rather there is this incredible battle between Bruce and the CEO about my performance. While they are battling, I simply return to the aircraft. I am a bit heartbroken.

Everyone returns to the aircraft, and we prepare to depart for home. Bruce returns to the seat next to me. I think he was just as surprised as me that I was emotional. His camouflaged efforts are working, my heart is tender. Bruce and I realized that the CEO is unaware of my skillset and my work ethic. He is running a very large business and doesn't have time to do the exhaustive work that Bruce has invested in me. Our company management team is made up of entrepreneurs which work in silos that are seldom shared among the team. Neither Bruce nor I held the CEO accountable for his uninformed complaints.

Bruce simply looked at me and asked, "Do you have a plan on how to fix this?"

I replied, "I will do what I do best. I will button-up what we have and get it implemented ASAP. Oh, and thank you for covering for me back there."

Bruce replied, "There are times where you will have to cover for yourself, but not today. Today people know that if anyone fights with you then they are fighting with us. They may win the fight, but we are all going to the hospital." Yet another Bruce-ism quote. (laughing)

It was hilarious. After only a couple of minutes on the aircraft, my spirit of hurt had transformed into a spirit of determination to exceed expectations and to do it immediately.

Christian Hebrew Study

As a 1st time book writer with a million pages to share, I decided to not consider researching the rules of what it takes to be a good author. I simply opened my word processing program that hopefully corrects all my inherited bad grammar while I share the stories of my life, life of those around me, life of those I love, and my latest understanding of the character of my Creator and Savior. Doing my best to be chronological, my apologies when it's not. Some have suggested that I write separate books compartmentalizing these three threads of life. I thought about it and no, I'm not going to do that. Let's tell it all at the same time until we are done.

All that know me, hold me in high regard as one of the weirdest but good-hearted people they know. That's good enough for me. If the Creator that gave me these words, is the only one to ever read it, that's good enough for me also. But, with all humility I ask that He at least reveal this book to my kids and those to whom I have done injustice during my path. Some of you, great injustice. My apologies with tears of regret.

The Christian Hebrew Study section is where I merge life and Bible with Hebrew. Teaching Adult Sunday School is one of the joys of my life. Impossible to exaggerate my commitment to return each week to reveal what has never been shared. From my methods of studying Hebrew, the supply of revelation cannot be contained within many lifetimes. I literally wake up each day to learn the next revelation. Glory!

It's the 2nd Sunday of 2022 and my Sunday School class has more than 20 people attending. Since the time I agreed to lead this class in November, I have been planning my course outline. I try to stay at least six weeks ahead of schedule. Remember, this is me, I am attending Saturday Bible studies with Christians that share the revelations provided by the original Hebrew text and then teaching Sunday School on Sunday's.

I have an agenda. My first agenda is to revive an adoration of Bible knowledge. Get people to spend more time studying their Bible than the one hour of church attendance each week. My 2nd agenda is to slowly, very slowly reveal God's Hebrew language and the depth of understanding it provides. To accomplish this, my first four weeks of study are the Book of Ruth. I spent one week on each Chapter. This book is nonconfrontational and packed with a depth of revelation from the Hebrew text that is not visible in the translations. The class loved it when they learned her name means Friend. The study of the Book of Friend was a blazing success. Many times, students were taking pictures of the PowerPoint slides that outlined the teaching.

A few weeks later I was privileged once again to speak at the Wednesday Christian Fellowship. I had just finished studying the life of Phineas, son of Eleazer, son of Aaron. Phineas's name translated to English means "Mouth of Serpent". We will be searching out Phineas in the next book of this series but just know that after that talk, people were talking. Phineas is a major character of the Old Testament, and his story is seldom discussed because of its graphic nature. I was able to redact the scriptures to make the talk family compliant, but the scriptures spoke for themselves. My pastor attended that night.

The Medina Volunteer Fire Department (MVFD) had training scheduled the following evening. Pastor and several others that attended the talk the previous night are members of MVFD. There was a moment when the pastor and I had some private time and all he could say was, "I don't know Mark, they don't teach that stuff at Seminary School." I wasn't sure how to take that, so I didn't reply. A few weeks later he would gift me his family's Pre-World War II Bible written in Hebrew. I will cherish it forever. It's priceless. Thank you, Pastor.

I have many friends that are pastors, and they are from various denominations. I am aware of the diversity of what is taught at Seminary School for these denominations. That said, a few of my pastor friends will confess that Bible knowledge is no different than any technical field. Bible research must continue throughout your ministry similar to continuing education for any other career.

Honor of Kings

My educational resume would be impressive to most. That said, I learned that nearly every character trait within me that was utilized to attain this education contributed to making it difficult to learn Hebrew. I know, that doesn't make sense but as we continue it will make perfect sense.

The next Hebrew word we will search out is Donkey. Oh, how I love this word and all its references in scripture. I know, you would have never guessed that the word Donkey would make it this high on the list, right? Well, by the time this chapter is finished, hopefully you will begin seeing the consistent increase of revelation in stories you already knew, and it will build a passion to learn the Hebrew letters.

If you ever owned a donkey then you know that in addition to possessing distinctive personality qualities, they also possess the instinctive nature to protect. This is why many farmers with herd animals usually have at least one donkey in the herd to protect the herd from predators. What is also very common is that the predator will generally attack the weakest animal in the herd, which is usually the goat's kid or the cow's calf or the pregnant mother. Rarely will the predator attack the ram or bull. The instinctive nature of the donkey is to protect the herd, especially the womb with a child or the young of the herd. Farmers know that a female donkey has more instinctive protective character than a male. There are several internet videos that reveal this instinctive nature.

Once again, let's recall what Jesus told us in Matthew 4:4.

Matthew 4:4 KJV: But he answered and said, It is written, Man shall not live by bread alone, but by every word that proceedeth out of the mouth of God (יהוה).

Notice that He didn't say by every verse, chapter, or book but by every word. Well, my research reveals approximately 25 instances of the word DONKEY in the original Hebrew text.

A couple of the most common stories where a donkey is included are when Mary, the mother of Jesus rode a donkey to Bethlehem and the other is when Jesus rode a donkey into Jerusalem which is commonly referred to as the triumphal entry. There are more occurrences but let's limit our research to these two occurrences.

The Hebrew word for a female donkey is Chmor (חמור). The definition of the letters that spell Chmor (חמור) is, "The Protection (ח) of the Womb (מ), of the Straight-up man with the Nail (ו), and the Prince (ר)." So, the noun of a female donkey in Hebrew tells us that it will protect the womb, Jesus during His time in the flesh (including the triumphal entry), and the Prince (Son of God).

The Same Story Again First, realize that these animals were named by Adam, right? Do you think Adam spoke Hebrew? Do you think he spent time learning the behavior of these animals before they were named? Surely, he did, right? So, Mary is riding the animal that God ordained from creation to be the protector of the womb of our Savior into Bethlehem.

The Same Story Again Picture your Savior riding into Jerusalem on a colt while we search out Matthew 21:2 and Zechariah 9:9.

Matthew 21:2 KJV: Saying unto them, Go into the village over against you, and straightway ye shall find an ass tied, and a colt with her: loose **them**, and bring **them** unto me.

Zechariah 9:9 KJV: Rejoice greatly, O daughter of Zion; shout, O daughter of Jerusalem: behold, thy King cometh unto thee: he is just, and having salvation; lowly, and **riding upon an ass** (חמור), **and upon a colt the foal** of an ass (אתנות).

This ***role of the donkey*** in the story of Jesus entering Jerusalem the week of the crucifixion is referred to as the "The Triumphal Entry" and has been retold with pictures and movies with many variations. My understanding of Matthew 21:2 and Zechariah 9:9 is that there are ***two*** donkeys entering Jerusalem. One is the mother, and the other is a colt (male, a female foal is called a filly), her foal following her which I believe Jesus is riding. Though the results of an internet search seem to be constantly changing, I have not been able to find a picture of this version of the story (which I find encouraging). I have not met many people aware that there were two donkeys entering Jerusalem during the triumphal entry.

The Same Story Again Occasionally when we exercise The *Honor of Kings,* we will reveal the findings of research and then share the details of the research for those that enjoy the *Honor of Kings*. There are always additional revelations in the research.

In our research we will reveal that the translation of the names of the departure and arrival cities traveled in these two stories will show that they traveled in opposite directions.

Mary and Joseph traveled from a guarded place to a place of fruitfulness.

Jesus traveled from fruitful place to a guarded place.

You can either skip to the next "***The Same Story Again***" or continue and participate in *The Honor of Kings* detailing the research of this revelation.

THE HONOR OF KINGS (Research – Optional)

A chiasm is the repetition of similar ideas in the reverse sequence.

To understand this chiasmic relationship requires understanding the Hebrew meanings of the names of the departure and arrival towns in these two stories. Enjoy the beauty of the Gospel that will be revealed (Gal גל) in the translation of the names of these towns.

Story #1 Mary Riding a Donkey from Nazareth to Bethlehem – Do you agree that it is interesting to learn that the town of Nazareth is not mentioned in the Old Testament? But there is a reference to the word Netzer in Isaiah 11:1.

Isaiah 11:1 KJV: And there shall come forth a **rod** (חטר) out of the stem of Jesse, and a Branch (Netzer or Natzer - ונצר) shall grow out of his roots:

It is interesting that the word "Branch" in Isaiah 11:1 is spelled with a capital "B". The Hebrew word for Branch in this verse is Natzer, and it means to watch or guard something that will bear fruit. The only other verse where Natzer is found is Proverbs 24:12.

Proverbs 24:12 KJV: If thou sayest, Behold, we knew it not; doth not he that pondereth the heart consider it? and he that keepeth (Netzer or Natzer - ונצר) thy soul, doth not he know it? and shall not he render to every man according to his works?

In Proverbs 24:12 Netzer is translated in the KJV as "keepeth" while other translations (NIV, NLT, EXB, etc) use guards or protects. Nonetheless, these two instances have a link to Jesus. Could this "Branch" from Netzar that "keepeth" my soul be a Nazarene? I think so.

We already know that Bethlehem translated means "The House of Bread". What many don't know is that the prior to being name of Bethlehem, the Bible referred to it as Ephratah which means "Fruitfulness".

Conclusion – Mary and Joseph are traveling from a place that guards or protects to the fruitful house of bread.

Story #2 Jesus Riding a Donkey from Bethphage, then Bethany to Jerusalem.

Mark 11:1 KJV: And when they came nigh to Jerusalem, unto Bethphage and Bethany, at the mount of Olives, he sendeth forth two of his disciples,

The Hebrew translation for Bethphage is "House of Unripe Figs", and for Bethany is "House of Figs", and for Jerusalem is "Foundation of Peace".

Conclusion – Jesus traveled from fruitfulness to a place of peace.

From the translation of the names of the cities it would appear they went in opposite directions. Glory to the King!

Isn't it interesting to learn that Jesus was in Bethany when He cursed the fig tree. He was in Bethany, the House of Figs, seeking fruit from a fig tree that had no fruitfulness, so He cursed it. Yes, I am familiar with the symbolism of Israel and figs, but in this story, I simply want to focus on the names of the cities. Until learning Hebrew, I was unaware that the name Bethany translated to "The House of Figs". Add that knowledge to all the fig tree symbolism of your past and glean new revelations.

The Same Story Again My apologies but this 15 seconds cannot be summarized. I pray this exercise of the *Honor of Kings* is as life changing for you as it was for me. Enjoy the reward of **AMAZING REVELATION** of scripture.

First, since we will be referencing these two stories so often, let's abbreviate the Joseph and Mary travels from Nazareth to Bethlehem by calling it the Mary story and likewise the triumphal entry as the Jesus story.

The Mary and Jesus stories are the first chiasmic stories we will research. It is very likely that a chiasmic relationship is something new for most. By the end of this book series, you will see that this is a common method where our Creator conceals incredible revelation. Know that all chiasmic stories often have many chiasmic comparisons. Let's identify other chiasmic relationships of these two stories.

- Mary story leaves a guarded place for a fruitful place.
  - Mary story is a journey to his birth.
    - Mary story has a mother and her son riding.
      - Mary Story has a father figure walking.
      - *Jesus Story does not have a father riding.*
    - Jesus story has the mother (donkey) and her son walking.
  - Jesus story is a journey to his death.
- Jesus story leaves a fruitful place for a guarded place.

Isn't it ironic that we do not have a chiasmic relationship because in the Jesus story the Father is missing? Chiasmic structures can be humorous as well as enlightening. Okay, so you see the task, we are looking for scriptural evidence that the Father is clearly present with His son at the triumphal entry. ***Impossible to exaggerate the privilege*** to be made aware to do the *Honor of Kings* and search out this matter. We are searching out information that we never considered to investigate. Just imagine the impact if we find this.

To find this concealed story we must approach the scriptures with complete bias. Ignore nothing as potential evidence. We are looking for evidence of something never found or even considered as necessary to be found. It's true, one could argue this isn't a pressing matter but consider all that changes in this story if we find that the Father entered Jerusalem with His Son while riding the mother donkey. Just the thought of it makes sense. I wouldn't let my son enter that environment without being by his side.

So first, I pray and rejoice that the desire for this effort is revealed to me. I expressed that this isn't something I find but rather something He must reveal. If He wants me to know, He must reveal it. I also know from personal experience and many experiences shared by friends, that when He reveals something, it is beautiful and magnificent.

Again, from my personal experience I have learned that few people were aware that there were two donkeys in the triumphal entry. When I learned of these two donkeys many years ago, I had never heard of a Biblical chiasmic story. Also, I didn't know Hebrew, so I didn't know the depth of the Father's language. Tasks like this were never on my radar. But now, when I re-read the triumphal entry, then research the original Hebrew, revelations are *SCREAMING* something that has been concealed from me my entire life. Now you get to search out what has been revealed to decide for yourself.

What is the scripture *SCREAMING*? It is screaming for me to correct the disparity of reverence between the role of the fathers in these two stories. While Joseph is perceived to have an unblemished participation, the Father bears the role of one that forsakes His Son.

In the story of Mary and Joseph traveling to Bethlehem for His birth, the role of Joseph as a father is without blemish. I won't fill this chapter with examples of highest praise and righteous character that are told and inferred about Joseph. We know the story well; almost all that know the Bethlehem story are aware of the beautiful fatherly role of Joseph during the birth of a child. Like all stories of a childbirth, the birth of Christ story is a time of celebration.

But wait! We are researching these two stories to find any evidence of participation of Jesus's Father in Heaven. Well, His role is not absent in the birth story. Without His participation, this story wouldn't exist.

Because Joseph did not live to witness the crucifixion, we are granted the privilege of providing our own conjecture of how we feel he would have handled it. I have never heard any negative conjecture of what Joseph would have done if he had lived to witness the crucifixion. Joseph rightfully gets positive press.

Jesus's real Father, our Father, did not get the privilege of being unavailable during His Son's crucifixion. Though our Father's participation in the story is described with a minimal number of scriptures, there is no lack of rhetoric and conjecture of those verses. What is the scripture *SCREAMING*? How does the understanding of scripture, and the rhetoric (conjecture) change if there is scriptural evidence that He physically entered Jerusalem with His son? Did Jesus's real Father experience and participate in the story of Jesus's death with as much respect that is given to Joseph in the story of His birth? Does the original Hebrew text provide untold revelation of this story? If we find clear evidence that the Father is in fact riding into Jerusalem with His son, then how does that impact the traditional passed-down teachings and scriptures of the triumphal entry and the events of the crucifixion story? Can the mere understanding that there are two donkeys make this big of a splash? Before reviewing the impact of these two donkeys in answering these questions, we must prepare by gleaning insight into Matthew 27:46.

Matthew 27:46 KJV: And about the ninth hour Jesus cried with a loud voice, saying, Eli, Eli, lama sabachthani? that is to say, *My God, my God, why hast thou forsaken me?*

Anyone who has attended church for a decade has heard multiple sermons of this verse. Certainly, almost every year during the week of the crucifixion. After forty years of church, I am quite certain there is no version of a sermon on this verse that I have not heard, and every sermon explains and consistently reveals that Jesus was forsaken by His Father on the cross. I would like to add 15 seconds into *The Same Story Again.* Let's reveal scripture that was concealed from me until late in life. Scripture that might have been spoken publicly but it just never made it on my radar. Let's add 15 seconds to the story we already know.

It seems that many times authors of books are burdened with sharing what cannot and should not be shared from behind a pulpit. Churches cannot schedule a risky sermon with potential that less than 100% of the congregation will agree. The pulpit is not for correcting passed down interpretations that we inherited from birth. Come on, Mark. You can't be serious. Think about it, few are aware that there is an organization that for centuries has exercised the authority of determining what books of the Bible are inspired. Every denomination has accepted this organization's finding as fact. Most of their changes to the "divine and inspired" took place before the modern generation was born. That organization determines what books are in our Canon, the Catholic Church. Well, my apologies, but let's do the *Honor of Kings*!

From birth I have always been taught that Christ was forsaken by His Father because He chose to become sin while on the cross and sin is not allowed in the presence of the Father. Until late in life I never even considered an alternative. So, even if we prove that the Father was with His son at the triumphal entry, it does not change that He is a father that forsakes his son, and we still deny Him the accolades we give to Joseph. Well, under those conditions, I don't want to find Him riding into Jerusalem as a loving Father only to reveal Him as a forsaking Father a few days later. Is there any ABSOLUTE SCRIPTURAL evidence to prove that He has never forsaken His son? We will deal with the ramifications of that understanding after it is proven, but first, is there SCRIPTURAL evidence that would prove His innocence?

The verse where Jesus expresses His Father has forsaken Him is Matthew 24:46. Let's review the event of verse 48 to determine if there is any concealed evidence to prove otherwise. The most crucial evidence is to realize that this verse provides details of an event took place after the supposed forsaking in Matthew 27:46. To be clear, prior to what is about to be revealed, the Father has supposedly already forsaken His son.

Matthew 27:48 KJV: And straightway one of them ran, and took a spunge, and filled it with vinegar, and put it on a reed, and gave him to drink.

Jesus is given a drink two verses after He is supposedly forsaken. Two verses after He takes this drink, He "yielded up the ghost". Now let's read that same incident as shared by the Gospel of John. (John 19:28-29)

John 19 KJV:

[28] After this, Jesus knowing that all things were now accomplished, *that the scripture might be fulfilled*, saith, I thirst.

[29] Now there was set a vessel full of vinegar: and they filled a spunge with vinegar, and put it upon hyssop, and put it to his mouth.

Verse 29 reveals that this is the same event mentioned in Matthew 27:48 though it does include the use of hyssop which we will search out later. Now let's look at verse 28 and notice the part of the scripture I have emphasized. So, just before His death He declares that to **FULFILL SCRIPTURE** He says that He is thirsty. Ok, I am certain that I know what scripture He fulfilled but FAR MORE IMPORTANT is to realize that He is still trying to make it clear that He is the Messiah. So, He went from being forsaken by His Father two verses ago and is once again fulfilling the Will of the Father. He is still working to leave evidence after His death of who He is. Hmm? Note: later we will prove that this event is all about the hyssop.

Now that we know He is still trying to provide evidence that He is the Messiah, let's consider if there is any evidence that would hint or prove that He is doing the same thing in Matthew 27:46 where we claim He is forsaken. Can we find any proof that would lend understanding that He consistently fulfilled the Will of His Father on the Cross. Is there proof that would reveal 24:46 as simply another act of Jesus to prove He is the Messiah just as He did in verse 48? Is there clear scriptural proof that the same Father in *Matthew 26:53-54* that Jesus proclaims would send more than twelve legends of Angels, is a Father that would NEVER FORSAKE HIS SON? Let's review Psalms 22:1 and Matthew 27:46 together.

Psalms 22:1 KJV: *My God, my God, why hast thou forsaken me?* why art thou so far from helping me, and from the words of my roaring?

Matthew 27:46 KJV: And about the ninth hour Jesus cried with a loud voice, saying, Eli, Eli, lama sabachthani? that is to say, *My God, my God, why hast thou forsaken me?*

For me, Psalms 22 is Holy Ground. It's a Psalm of David and it might be the most powerful of all Psalms. A Psalm quoted by Christ while on the cross. There are many public videos of sermons available that provide a view of why Christ quoted this Psalm. I have yet to find a video teaching of Psalm 22 that defends the Good, Good, Father by proving He would never forsake His Son.

I won't attempt to estimate the percentage of Christians that are unaware that Jesus is called the Son of David (Luke 18:38-39). There are many scriptures confirming that the Lord loved David. There is a common phrase "David the beloved" that is almost always quoted when preaching about David. That said, the phrase "David, the beloved" is not in the Bible. The Hebrew translation of the word David is "beloved". Yes, just like Jonah means Dove, David means Beloved. For me, knowing his name is Beloved adds to the stories of his life and once again makes me ponder past understanding. David is not just called by the title "Beloved", but his name is "Beloved". Everywhere you see the word David you can substitute it with Beloved. Did I repeat myself? Did I repeat myself? (smile)

Eight times in the New Testament God refers to Jesus as "beloved son". It seems appropriate that Jesus, the beloved son, would quote Beloved's words from Psalms 22:1?

I am very confident that John was aware of Beloved's Psalm that Jesus quoted and obviously he was aware of the scripture that was fulfilled. Most importantly, is this enough evidence to consider that Matthew 27:46 was for the same purpose as Matthew 27:48? Was He fulfilling His Father's Will prior to Matthew 27:46 and then forsaken in verse 46 and then returned to His Father's will in verse 48? Is Psalms 22:1 enough to render the Good, Good, Father NOT GUILTY of forsaking His Son? Is there more evidence? Yes, I believe every verse of Psalms Chapter 22 has more evidence. Let's search out verses 16-18.

Psalms 22:16-18 KJV: [16] For dogs have compassed me: the assembly of the wicked have inclosed me: they pierced my hands and my feet.

[17] I may tell all my bones: they look and stare upon me.

[18] They part my garments among them, and cast lots upon my vesture.

Yes, King Beloved (David) plays many roles in the scriptures. He is the only appointed King, a priest, a prophet, and a Psalmist. Surely you agree that Psalm 22 can be viewed as another effort of the Messiah to reveal Himself to those that did not recognize Him. We showed earlier in the first chapter that Psalms 22:8 is one of the verses where the Hebrew root word for Reveal (Gal גל) is used. Several translations have a footnote for the first word of this verse that tells us the word is literally "***Roll***". So, the first two words in the original Hebrew text are "*Roll Yahweh*". Also, there are two Hebrew words in this verse that are only used once in the Bible. My understanding of the Hebrew in this verse is "*Reveal the Father by Him Rolling Away the Stone and Delivers His Son and Rescues His Son Because He Delights in Him*".

Psalms 22:8 KJV: He ***trusted*** (גל) ***on the LORD*** (יהוה) that he would deliver him: let him deliver him, seeing he delighted in him.

I believe that if this evidence were provided in a trial by jury, the Father would be found NOT GUILTY of forsaking His son. The Good, Good, Father of my Savior is Righteous and Holy.

Now that my Father is not a forsaking father I have a new problem. The story I was always told is that the Father forsook His son in verse 46 because according to Paul's writing in 2 Corinthians 5:21, Jesus became sin. I have always understood that Jesus is forsaken by His Father in verse 46 because this is the moment that He became sin. I was taught that verse 46 fulfills Paul's writings in 2 Corinthians 5:21. My understanding is that He is forsaken because His Father will not allow sin in His presence. This is passed down understanding of scripture that existed before I was born. I grew up with this understanding which I consider to be "bedrock of doctrine" of almost all churches.

2 Corinthians 5:21 KJV: For he hath made him to be sin for us, who knew no sin; that we might be made the righteousness of God in him.

There is no doubt that Jesus became sin while on the cross. The question is when? There is clear evidence that He didn't become sin in verse 46 and there is clear evidence that the Father didn't forsake Him. When did Jesus who knew no sin become sin? How is it possible for Him to become sin and not be forsaken by His Father? What is the exact moment that He became sin? I believe this question becomes easier to answer if you participate in a silly exercise. I am not joking; you must go with me on this. This silly exercise will hopefully help you see things that you are not accustomed to seeing. I hope to prove that you have already seen the answer to this question. Yes, you have read it but simply didn't recognize it.

Here we go. (smile) Ask yourself or anyone you know if they have ever eaten a Jiffe peanut butter sandwich and almost everyone will answer yes. I can prove that nobody has ever eaten a Jiffe peanut butter sandwich because Jiffe doesn't exist, it's actually called **Jiff**. Well, our mind has been conditioned to hear and accept what we have perceived for so long. The exercise is to simply make us aware that it is human nature to overlook what we read and see, and replace it with what has been repeatedly viewed and heard. If you fell for that, then you are likely going to enjoy finding that you have already read the answer to the question "When did Jesus become sin?".

In the first chapter of this book, we shared a fictitious story about an atheist named Bob asking a question to his Christian friend Jiff (smile). This time read Bob's argument and question, then read Jiff's answer which explains clearly when Jesus became sin.

Bob, a former Christian, and now outspoken atheist was talking to Jiff, a Christian brother from his past, *"Let me make sure I understand and don't interrupt. You still believe that if Adam and Eve would not have eaten from the tree, that they would still be alive in the garden. You claim that death is the penalty of sin, so if you don't eat the tree then you have no sin and live forever. But you also believe in a Savior that died that never sinned. You can't have it both ways. If the penalty of sin is death, then how can you claim that your Savior, who died, was without sin? I never understood it. Those two stories contradict each other and it's ridiculous for the churches to think they can have it both ways. You must pick a side, either the penalty of sin is death, or it isn't. How can you explain it?"*

Jiff replies, *"Bob, I love the question. Please don't interrupt because I think I have an answer for you. The Book of Matthew 26:53-54 tells of the situation in the Garden of Gethsemane where Peter cuts off the ear of a man trying to arrest Jesus. Jesus miraculously heals the man's ear then declares to Peter that He could pray to His Father and He would immediately send more than twelve legions of Angels. Then Jesus asked Peter that if He did that then how would the scriptures be fulfilled?*

Jesus didn't die because of any sin committed. He willfully stayed on the cross until His death to fulfill the scriptures. He literally chose not to come off the cross. If He had committed one sin, then He would have justly died on the cross for His own sin. His willingness to stay on the cross, and His choice to accept the penalty of sin, all resulted in His death. His willful death is the sole act of Him becoming sin. His only participation in the sin story is His death, the penalty of sin. His death is synonymous with Him becoming sin."

Yes, I took a big risk that many people would read that conversation and totally discard the rest of the book. A risk I had to take to over-rule a lifetime of doctrine embedded in passed down teaching. A doctrine I taught to my kids. That said, this is an amazing moment for those that understand the path we just took. No, we aren't nearly done.

The Same Story Again I must soak in this for one more paragraph. I heard "the forsaken story" my whole life, what's one more paragraph going to hurt. Isn't it awesome to have a valid explanation of 2 Corinthians 5:21 that does not require us to view the Father as one that forsakes His Son? Isn't Psalms 22 an amazing 15 seconds? Likewise, isn't it refreshing to know that Jesus said those words in verse 46 and there was no strife in the Father's house. Can you imagine Jesus telling His bride to come and visit His Father and then the bride says, "I don't want to meet your dad that has forsaken you?"

The "Forsaking Father Doctrine" is so embedded that many will still cleave to it. I can't and won't go back to that. I have repented and will never entertain that doctrine again. I will tell the story in a book and publish it for the whole world to see. (smile)

Glory to the King!

Hey kids! Sadly, your dad isn't as weird as you think!

I could end this lesson right here, right? Why can't I just say that there were two donkeys entering Jerusalem and Jesus was on the colt and His Father on the colt's mother? Boom! The lesson is done and let's move on. I just can't! I feel that would resemble a style of learning that I inherited from birth. I have passion to prove that my loving Father was with His Son for the entire week of the triumphal entry. I am convinced that what I am looking for is concealed in these two donkeys. I am **DETERMINED** to prove that not only is my Father not one that forsakes but He is also one that will carry your burden. I must prove that Jesus's loving Father was with Him the entire way.

Just the day before, Jesus declared that His Father would dispatch more than 12 legions of Angels. Now we know that never changed. I have a new vision that the entire crucifixion story took place with His loving Father by His side. This would be 100% contrary to the passed down traditions that existed before my birth.

Once again, there are many variations of this story but as you can see, in Matthew 21:2 Jesus says to bring **THEM** (both donkeys).

Matthew 21:2 KJV: Saying unto them, Go into the village over against you, and straightway ye shall find an ass tied, and a colt with her: loose _**them**_, and bring _**them**_ unto me.

Now let's look at Zechariah 9:9 one more time and see that it also prophecies of two donkeys.

Zechariah 9:9 KJV: Rejoice greatly, O daughter of Zion; shout, O daughter of Jerusalem: behold, thy King cometh unto thee: he is just, and having salvation; lowly, and **riding upon an ass (חמור), and upon a colt the foal of an ass (אתנות)**.

Now notice that the two Hebrew words translated as donkey are not spelled the same. Jesus is riding on her colt (a male foal). This verse provides the spelling of a female (חמור) donkey and a male (אתנות) colt. Let's search out the spelling of each donkey. I am convinced that what I am trying to find is concealed within the original Hebrew letters that spell these two nouns. First, let's search out the male colt.

There are many ways to apply the definition of the Hebrew letters that spell the male colt (אתנות). My favorite is:

> _"The Father's (א) Covenant (ת)_
> _is the life (נ) of the straight-up man with the nail (ו) and the cross (ת)."_

The definition of the Hebrew letters for this Word adds revelation to Jesus's many references that He does the will of His Father. The definition makes it clear that His Father's covenant lives, and that Jesus's life and crucifixion fulfilled that covenant.

What is also interesting about this word is that the first two letters spell the word Et (את). These are the **FIRST** letter and the **LAST** letter of the Hebrew alphabet. Yet another reference for **First and Last** not available in the translations. Later we will search out the word Et (את) but for now know that in The Book of the Revelation, Jesus refers to Himself as The Alpha and the Omega. Alpha and Omega are the first and last letters of the Greek alphabet, the Hebrew equivalent is the Alef (א) and the Tav (ת). The word Et (את) is like Jesus's signet ring, His stamp. Also, know that the letter Tav (ת) can mean either Covenant or Cross. Now, let's add this understanding to our definition.

"Jesus (את) is the Father's (א) Covenant (ת),
His life (ב) as straight-up man with the nail (ו) and on the cross (ת)
is the Covenant."

Yay! I knew it! The definition of Hebrew spelling of the colt confirms that my Savior was riding the colt. I am confident that we will find the Father on the colt's mother.

We have already defined the Hebrew letters of the female donkey (חמור) but let's do it again with the intent of finding our Loving Father. The definition of the Hebrew letters that spell donkey is:

"The Protection (ח) of the Womb (מ)[1], the Straight-up man with the Nail (ו)[2], and the Prince (ר)[3]".

So, the female donkey protects three things 1) Jesus's birth, 2) His life as a straight up man and on the cross with the nail, and 3) His resurrection.

I'm convinced. I only required a hint of proof, and this was beyond that. My Father is a Loving Father. A humble Loving Father that protected His son. He never left His side. The last letter of this word proves that ***He Protected Knowing He Would Resurrect His Son***. He was prepared to send more than twelve legends of Angels upon request.

My Savior willfully bore the shame and penalty of death without sin. By His Own Hand He bore the mockery and shame of a Roman cross because He loved the World. His Father bore the pain of watching the innocent blood of His murdered Son on the same Earth that He created.

<u>Spoiler alert!</u> Later we will search out the 1st Hebrew word ever spoken by the Father. That word means "IN THE RESURRECTION".

I hope you are as convinced as I am that the ***Good, Good, Father*** is sitting on that Donkey and leading the way for His Son to be victorious over Sin and Death! I've only recently seen the story in this light. I could re-read this chapter every day! Oh, how I love this! And all of it is scripture-based! No conjecture!

<u>The Same Story Again</u> While we are seeing the Father in a renewed reverence, I believe this is a awesome time to share my understanding of the 3rd Commandment.

Exodus 20:7 KJV: Thou shalt not take the name of the LORD thy God in vain (לשוא); for the LORD will not hold him guiltless that taketh his name in vain.

The Hebrew word translated as vain is Lashua (לשוא) and I believe would be better translated as futility, the act of making His name pointless, useless, small, and insignificant. The definition of the Hebrew letters is "The Authority That Leads (ל) to the Destruction (שׁ) of The Straight Up Man With the Nail (ו) and His Father (א).

Nobody does a better job of making the Father insignificant than His enemy. I am personally guilty and forgiven for making His name small. The origin of my ability to make His name small originated in the garden. I now realize that the enemy had nearly 2,000 years of influence since the resurrection and my birth. I am convinced that the enemy is the source of the passed down deception that my Father was absent during the triumphal entry. He is the deceiver that hid the protecting mother of the colt. He is the deceiver that portrayed my Father as one that would forsake His Son.

I am on a mission to search out the deceptions of passed down traditions. Yes, I have become aware of many and uncovering more! One Word at a time! Matthew 4:4.

Hey kids, I prefer you search out everything shared in this chapter until it is your story and not just one that you read. Oh, how I wish I had known this when you were young.

Glory to the King!

Chapter 5

Aebi (אהבי), Ruth (רות) – Friend

LIFE

Until knowing Bruce and his family I had never understood how people express that someone is "a brother from another mother". I have never had one of those. I am grateful that Bruce exercised his authority as my brother many times to shame me of my moral understandings as well as my judgmental attitudes. I can only estimate that this story takes place in December 2005.

Bruce's grandmother was the dean at one of the local Bible colleges and she played a huge impact on the family's spiritual and Biblical understanding. By now, I am realizing that Bruce is passing that understanding to a wayward brother that shows up on the scenes of life.

It was just another day, and my phone rang, it was my ex-wife, the mother of my two girls. The content of the conversation is irrelevant. What matters is how I was emotionally impacted during and after the call. Remember, Bruce doesn't like anybody he shares life with to have a bad day. I am learning over and over how sincere he is. The man seems incapable of telling a lie. I am also learning how grossly he is misunderstood. That broken volume knob and outspoken willingness to use it creates a huge misunderstanding of the man that lives within.

I get off the phone and my day is now controlled by the irritations of conflict. Bruce and I both had a vulgar mouth in those days but truly wish that if this story is ever retold that those words would either be bleeped-out or just simply not included so that people that need this story won't be hindered. The spirit of what takes place doesn't require revealing the cursing. I am still negotiating "life after a near death" experience and learning that my Savior's fuse to reach judgement is very long. His ultimate plan and purpose are never-ending.

With that passionate knobbed voice Bruce asks me, "Dude, who was that?"

I reply, "My ex-wife."

Now the sermon begins. No, this isn't the first sermon. By now I have learned that Bruce's sermons are without interruption and generally last for more than an hour. (laughing) They also have a hidden agenda. He wants the pain of hearing his viewpoint to be so great, that you never want to experience the same sermon twice. Hence, almost every time he talks, he doesn't stop until he is confident that the wires in the head of his new-found brother have been sufficiently re-terminated to their proper place. I am eternally grateful.

It is impossible to retell the much needed, low cost, and unsolicited sermon. But an hour later and with remarkable understanding it is impossible to argue that my Savior wants me to love my ex-wife more today than ever in my life. I challenge even Alex Kendrick to write better stories than the masterpieces I am privileged to hear and retell.

I remember one of the "Bruce-isms" of the sermon. He and I talked for hours about his childhood. Then after just two or three stories of my childhood, it becomes clear that it's not to be shared, it's like an old-fashioned juke box that only plays when you want it to. That said, Bruce always defended my deceased dad's role in my childhood stories but this time he said, "Man, for the first time, I want to dig up your dad and take him behind the woodshed then bring him back." (smile)

This is my friend! It's amazing to witness how many people have access to this guy and somehow, I am his friend. What's wrong with you people? Your loss is my gain! The naive wisdom of being his friend makes me feel good about me.

The love Bruce is describing is that "Love Your Neighbor" stuff you read about in the Bible. And, truly by loving my remarried ex-wife, I will be healed, and my kids will be healed. I begin a new prayerful journey and my destination is to experience the opportunity to properly apologize to her for walking away from my vows made before God. Yes, of course, that day comes in a *miraculous* way many years later. Our divorce was finalized on February 24, 1995. Here I am more than ten years later praying that I could love her more now than I had ever loved her before.

It's April 2016, and one of my daughter's closest friends is getting married. The wedding was awesome, and we are now headed to the outside reception area. Lisa and I look around and she pics a table. We both set our cellphones down and walked over to the serving area. We are friends and not family, so we waited and allowed lots of folks to go ahead of us. The entire time we had our backs to the table, and we finally made our plate and when we turned around, we noticed that my ex-wife and her husband were sitting at our table alone.

We let them know that those were our phones and that we are okay with sitting together if they are okay with it. They agreed and we ate and began having conversations.

It's twenty-one years since my divorce from my 1ˢᵗ wife and almost eleven years since Lisa and I started praying for the people we had hurt in our past. My daughter visits the table and openly declares how awkward it is to see us sitting at the same table. She has the personality to get away with that. Lisa and I both know that this is the miracle we had been waiting for.

Finally, I got the nerve and asked, "I need you guys to grant me permission to say something. Yes, it requires your permission." They agreed and I continued but now my voice is cracking, and my eyes are tearing as I looked at my ex-wife and said, "I'm so sorry. No woman deserves to be treated the way I treated you. It would be a gift to know that you forgive me for a long list of things that I don't care to itemize."

You could see that she was surprised and grateful as she replied, "You are forgiven."

Glory to the King!

Looking back to that October 2005 sermon, I realize that sermon had more benefits than just the healing of everyone involved. Bruce taught on the sanctity of marriage and many other things that he learned while growing up at home. It registered! I will never again be a man that breaks his vows. The man that broke his promise would never be that man again. How many times do I say, "Thank you, Bruce".

I can only pray that my novice writing skills are not a distraction for the ones that I love. They all witnessed a portion of the story but are not aware of its daily development at the expense of such an eternal investment.

LIFE

Let's step further back in time. It's the summer of 1975, I am 16 years old and working at a local hometown restaurant named Riddle's Restaurant. I must shout thank you to the late Darryl Riddle who treated me like a son. I could write an entire book on the events of that summer.

There was a very old man named Fred Lutz that came into the restaurant daily. Fred had to be at least 80 years old. Just seeing him was evidence of the miracle that he is still alive. Fred was obviously born with a simple mind, and I can only assume that as he got older it became simpler.

Maybe five years later I would visit another nearby small town and witness my imagination of Fred in his 30's. I'm an official at a high school basketball game and at every moment that the gym floor was available this guy was running around the gym doing his best to bounce the ball and make a hoop. Each time he showed outward emotions of having done something cool, the entire home crowd would cheer. They would cheer louder for this guy than they did for their own kids. Yes, the man was special but more importantly he was loved, protected, adored, and adopted by the entire town.

I can only estimate it's ten years later and Fred has passed. I am driving down old Hwy 378 and passing the road where Fred lived and notice that the town has renamed the road Fred Lutz Road. I have fond memories of Fred sitting with the town folk at that restaurant. What a gift to have known Fred. My hometown folk memorialized Fred by renaming the street where he lived. Great job!

Fred Lutz Road

Christian Hebrew Study

Saturday Bible studies are amazing, but they are also content based. To share a typical Saturday would be like documenting a Bible study. Soon after learning Hebrew, my personal understanding of Matthew 4:4 led me to begin studying the Bible one word at a time. It resembles studying by subject but when you include the impact of Hebrew it is clearly a "Word Study" and not a "Topic Study".

Within the first month of attending these Saturday studies I became friends with one of the men that led the study, Micah. Micah and his family lead the worship on Saturdays. He is an amazing Christian with a passion for Biblical and Hebrew study. During our Saturday visits I shared and invited the group to attend my Sunday School class. Micah, James, and a few others took me up on the offer and showed up. None of them lived closer than 30 minutes away and their attendance and support was appreciated.

It is February 2022, and our Sunday School class has finished the Ruth study which included several strategic Hebrew words that added more depth of understanding than any had seen before. The Ruth study was a huge success that attracted more members to attend the class. Our highest attendance is now forty-four. Just five weeks ago, there were only six.

The next topic I chose for Sunday School was the story of Samson. Before teaching the first lesson about Samson, I already had the entire course outlined. This would be a seven-week study. The first week was planned to be a show of passion. For the first time I was intentionally introducing conflict with the traditional teachings passed down. I am not certain from where the traditional story was passed down, but I have ideas. My first familiarity with the passed down traditions of the Samson story was learned by watching a 1961 film when I was a child. My Hebrew studies provided evidence contrary to these traditions.

The first week of teaching the story of Samson was my first willful objection to traditional church teachings. The class flowed as planned and at the close of the lesson I made it very clear that over the next six weeks we will prove that Samson is not a womanizer but rather a story of an Appointed Judge sent by our creator to teach us about the Power of God. Yes, the entire class politely expressed that they couldn't wait to see my proof and nobody, including the Pastor's wife, was willing to join me in my stance.

Think about it, why would God include four chapters in the Book of Judges to reveal sexual immorality of the last judge of the book. A man that *He has appointed from birth*. Once you eliminate that this is not a story to encourage modern day womanizers to repent and be saved, then you can begin to see the revelations of the prophetic views which I believe to be God's purpose. Okay, do you need more? There are three women in the Samson story 1) the Philistine woman at Timnah, 2) the harlot and 3) Delilah.

The woman from Timnah was Samson's fiancé. Samson was betrothed but the marriage was never consummated. Samson never married. The Hebrew translation for Philistines is "Trespassers". The Hebrew translation for Timnah is "An Appointed Place". In Judges 15:6 it tells us that the woman's father was a Timnite. The translation of Timnite is "A Remnant". The summary of these translations tells us that Samson went to an Appointed Place to get a Bride from a Remnant of the Trespassers. Sound familiar?

The Bible does not declare Samson to be a womanizer, man's interpretations do that. The Bible provides the truth, but it is hidden in the translations of the Hebrew nouns. Yes, the harlot and Delilah stories further support the fact that God ordained Samson to be a Nazarite from Birth and that his life story would represent The Power of God. What? Do you need more?

Besides our misunderstanding of who the harlot and Delilah represent, there are many more God ordained hints for us to recognize in Samson's life. Like the Power of God, Samson's life resembles the timeline across millenniums of Bible history. Consider that Samson visited "The Cleft in the Rock" just like

Moses. Consider that Samson killed 3,000 when he left the Cleft of the Rock to battle the Philistines just as 3,000 died when Moses, who God placed in the Cleft of the Rock, came down from the mountain and discovered Israel serving the golden calf. Consider that 3,000 watched from the roof (weren't killed) as Samson presented his last physical demonstration of the Power of God just like 3,000 were saved on the Day of Pentecost. We will share more in upcoming chapters. To be continued.

Honor of Kings

It's only appropriate to share 15 seconds of understanding of what it is like to be a friend of God in scripture. Can you imagine the Word of God declaring you to be His friend? Unfathomable! Well, there are several examples of God's friends. So many that I will not proclaim to be capable of naming all of them.

For me, the most boldly declared friends of God are the twelve disciples. In addition to having the title "The Twelve Disciples" they are also eternally memorialized in the wall of New Jerusalem.

Revelation 21:14 KJV: And the wall of the city had twelve foundations, and in them the names of the twelve apostles of the Lamb.

There are some friends of God that came as a surprise to me when I learned the closeness of their friendship. There should be no debate that if your name is written on the gates of New Jerusalem, then you are one of God's closest friends.

Revelation 21:12 KJV: And had a wall great and high, and had twelve gates, and at the gates twelve angels, and names written thereon, which are the names of the twelve tribes of the children of Israel:

The stories of the twelve sons of Jacob range from brotherly love to extreme family dysfunctionality. The Bible tells of the mischief of these men. I can quickly recall the sinful stories of Rueben, Simeon, Levi, Judah, and Benjamin. That said, I can also recall the amazing story of Joseph. My point here is that though the sons of Israel don't require an introduction, the books that share their most amazing stories are no longer in the Canon, our Bible. We can easily search the Bible and read the embarrassment of Rueben but what we don't know is the amazing stories of Rueben. Those stories are shared in what is now called historical, non-Biblical text. I have read those stories. Stories equally as amazing as those of the twelve apostles and provide understanding to their names being memorialized in Revelation 21:12.

There are many Biblical references to friends of God.

James 2:23 KJV: And the scripture was fulfilled which saith, Abraham believed God (יהוה), and it was imputed unto him for righteousness: and he was called the Friend of God (יהוה).

Isaiah 41:8 KJV: But thou, Israel, art my servant, Jacob whom I have chosen, the seed of Abraham my friend (אהבי).

Ruth 4:10 KJV: Moreover Ruth (את-רות) the Moabitess, the wife of Mahlon, have I purchased to be my wife, to raise up the name of the dead upon his inheritance, that the name of the dead be not cut off from among his brethren, and from the gate of his place: ye are witnesses this day.

The Same Story Again Once again we have more than one Hebrew word translated into the same English word. Notice that the Hebrew word referenced with Abraham is not the same as Ruth whose name means Friend.

Note to my kids that I pray will read this one day. *Come on kids, your dad simply did not know this while you were in the house. Whatever version of this movie you have watched during my life, simply add these 15 seconds to the movie and purchase another ticket.* My apologies for the personal insertion.

Ruth's name in Ruth 4:10 (את-רות) provides another intro to the Hebrew word Et (את). Imagine yourself at church, the worship has just ended, and the Pastor gets behind the pulpit and says, "If you will turn with me into the Word of God (יהוה) to the Book of Friend chapter four. We will begin reading in verse ten. This is the first time that Friend's name is preceded with the First and the Last (את) stamp of our Savior. Prior to this verse, Friend's name was not preceded with His stamp. Notice also that this is the verse where Boaz declares that he has purchased her." Nope, though it is 100% accurate, in my life that has never been shared behind a pulpit. I know, you don't know anything about this "Jesus" stamp that exists throughout the Old and New Testament! I am only aware of one English Translation that includes it.

So, we have two people in the Bible referred to as a friend of God (יהוה). One is Abraham whom we know well, and the other is Ruth (רות), the Moabitess. Most Christians are not aware of the origin of a Moabitess. A Moabitess is a woman from Moab which is a city named after the incestual

relationship between Lot and his oldest daughter. Moab is synonymous for Sin.
Ruth is not from the tribes of Israel but was married to Mahlon whose mother
and father were both from Bethlehem. Now let's research the definition of the
Hebrew letters of these two Hebrew words translated as Friend.

The word translated as friend in the Abraham story is Aebi. The
definition of the word derived from the Hebrew letters is "God (א) Reveals (ה)
His House (ב) Where His Hands do Mighty Deeds (י)."

Isn't that exactly what Yahweh (God יהוה) used Abraham for? I will
bless them that bless you and curse them that curse you. Pretty sure that was a
personal promise to Abraham and his seed. I am grafted into the seed of
Abraham; therefore, those promises are for me as well. Glory to the King!
Ruth's name translated to English is the word, Friend. The definition
derived from the Hebrew letters is, "The Prince of Heaven (ר) is the Straight-up
Man with the Nail (ו) that fulfilled His Covenant (ת)." There are many
acceptable variations of the revelation sentence for the word Friend.

Ruth the Moabitess is a gentile woman from the land of sin. She is the
Great Grandmother of King Beloved (David).

Chapter 6

Abn (אבן) - Stone, Tzur (צור) – Rock

LIFE

I can only remember that I was in 3rd grade. It's likely 1968. We lived on St Joseph Street in Lafayette, Louisiana. Our housekeeper (NOT MAID) was a lady we called Ms. Mable. Ms. Mable is a Saint. She is old enough to be my grandmother and is literally a twin of Aunt Jemima on those syrup bottles. At the time of this story, I can only estimate she has been our housekeeper for three years. She has lasted longer than any in the past. Ms. Mable was with us during the darkest times of our family. I am old now, old enough to know that many of the greatest stories of life have painful origins. I am also old enough to have witnessed the unnecessary extreme cultural response to these types of stories, so very little of that pain will be shared.

I was Ms. Mable's favorite. She loved all of us, but she nicknamed me "My Poopsy". She called everyone else by their name but me, I'm her Poopsy. I came home from school that day and Ms. Mable made me a bowl of cereal and had to use the rest of the milk. Dad got home and wanted a cup of coffee and Ms. Mable told him we were out of milk because she gave the last of it to Poopsy with some cereal. Well, let's just say that Ms. Mable felt responsible for my dad's reaction to the news.

Years later, I estimate it was the summer of 1986 and my wife and I are driving through Lafayette on the way to her parents who live in Broussard. I literally get this familiar feeling from God. I tell my wife that God just told me to go see Ms. Mable. I drop her off at her moms and head to Ms. Mable's house on Lafayette St.

I had not seen Ms. Mable since I was 14 years old and truly had no idea if she was still alive. I am stunned to see the changes in her neighborhood, Lafayette was a growing town. When I got to her home there were vehicles parked on both sides of the road. I found a spot and walked to her house where there were several men talking in her fenced-in front yard. It was obvious they were a bit surprised to see a white man open the fence.

They were about to tell me that I can't use the front door when I interrupted, "I know, the couch blocks the front door, and you have to knock on the back door to get in."

One of the men replied, "Yes, that's right, can we help you?"

I replied, "Hello, I'm Mark, Ms. Mable was my housekeeper when I was young. Is she still alive?"

He replied, "Yes." as they all followed me to the back door.

I knocked on the door and her daughter, Delores, opens the door, "Hello Poopsy, what are you doing here?"

I replied, "I came to see Ms. Mable."

There were about 50 people in the yard and house. I have no idea how old you must be to recognize you are walking into a situation. Why didn't I realize that there wasn't supposed to be anybody home? I have visited family in my past and there would be only one person on the property. Why didn't I realize I am visiting 80-year-old Ms. Mable and there are fifty people on the property? How naïve can a person be?

Delores invites me into the house and now I can hear Ms. Mable crying with a loud cry. She is wailing.

Ms Mable sees me and is screaming, "Oh my God, it's my Poopsy. My Poopsy is here." She continues yelling as she walks towards me, "My Poopsy is here. Oh my God." As she hugs me, she asked, "Why are you here Poopsy?"

No kidding, the conversation begins with asking me why I am there. On the drive to her house, I did not picture this playing out this way. I pictured laughter and celebration and food. I pictured her in a wheelchair and me getting her a drink. I pictured me having a chance to be nice to a very old lady to whom I am in great debt. I imagined lots of life's questions and hugs and then I would leave.

Well, I couldn't lie so I told her, "Mom, I was driving through town and God told me to come see you."

Now Ms. Mable is really screaming, "Did y'all hear that. My Poopsy is here and he doesn't know why we are all here. He doesn't know! Oh my God, he doesn't know. You hear that, Delores? He doesn't know. God sent my Poospsy to see me on the day that I am burying my husband. My God is so good to me!" And she continues wailing.

As I write the story, I literally must stop and try to find words to express that moment. I recall that I was still too immature to recognize it for what it really is. Sure, I recognized the miraculous of it all and His participation in all of it. I just couldn't fathom the enormity of the moment. It's not that it is true, it's just that it surrounded me. The moment was too big. My presence in that room was a visible miracle. Ms. Mable looked at me and talked about me as though I was a miracle.

The visit was very short, and I stepped out to give the family their privacy. To this day I feel that I didn't show my adoration and love to her and the family. I think it's because I owe her so much. The men that followed me to the back door were still there and I can only assume they heard her words. One of them says, "You're Poopsy?"

I replied, "Yes."

He said, "Look around, she has one daughter, couple of grandkids, several brothers, sisters, in-laws, and nephews and all she ever talks about is you. What happened? We know something happened, but her lips are sealed."

I hope I was able to disguise how much I was struggling keeping it all together. But, somehow, I knew exactly what he was talking about. I looked at him and said, "She never got over it?"

He invited me to have a seat as I told them about the cereal. That was the only punishment that Ms. Mable believed was her fault. I told the man; you must let her know that I am okay. Everyone is okay. I know Ms. Mable is one of God's precious children. It is a long story. The time with them was far shorter than it sounds.

After the story I drove back to the in-laws. Once again, I realize how easy it is for each of us to view monumental experiences of someone else's life as today's news and quickly forgotten.

To simply describe Ms. Mable as a rock in my life would be a gross understatement. The truth is that everything I had learned good about life was taught to me by Ms. Mable. I had two amazing grandfathers, but Ms. Mable was there every day. God bless all that she loves, I am eternally in debt to them all.

Thank you, Ms. Mable!
I am old and still cry happy tears thinking about you.

Christian Hebrew Study

Saturday Bible studies are still amazing! Impossible to express the added revelations concealed in the Hebrew text of common Bible stories. Also, my personal commitment to watching amazing Bible Study videos posted by people that know Hebrew is consuming my spare time. I find that large percentages of the information I watch become a part of me and are immediately available for total recall. No, that's not a function of the brain but rather a condition of the heart. These stories and understandings simply become a part of me. I can't explain the psychology of whether that is possible, I just know this is not a function of me being smart. I truly believe anyone could do it. That said, you will not likely find anyone on the internet that shares my views on the story of Samson but everyone I teach has become a believer in what I am sharing. Iron sharpens iron.

It is now March 2022, and our Sunday School class is finishing the Story of Samson in the Book of Judges. We had special guests. Lisa's son and his fiancé are with us! Yay! What a treat to teach in their presence. What a joy to watch as God chooses to reveal Himself as The Power of God in the Samson story. Everyone that previously believed the passed-down traditions during the first week now know the scriptural evidence and that Samson was a righteous judge, appointed by God to reveal His Power.

The Samson story is in the Book of Judges chapters 13-16. Here are more 15-second revelations to add to the story. The second woman in Samson's story was the harlot. It says that Samson went in unto the harlot, but does that mean they had sex? Is this really a sex story? Is there anything that we can search out within the harlot story that could possibly conceal that this is a Power of God story? Yes, it tells us that while He was in the harlot's house that the trespassers (Philistines) were told that Samson was there. This provides the impression that Samson was betrayed just as Christ was betrayed. Oh wait, did I just connect a man inside of a harlot's house to our Savior? Jesus declared that He came only for the lost sheep of the house of Israel. This is the same Israel that God gave a bill of divorcement because they were whoring after other gods (Judges 2:17). Jeremiah 3:8 tells us that the house of Israel was a harlot, and that Judah played the harlot. So, like Jesus's story, Samson was betrayed, and they waited at the gate to kill him.

Is there more? Yes! Just as the Gospel of Jesus opened the door for all nations, the Jew first and then the gentile, Samson leaves the harlots house and with the strength that only God could provide, rips the gate off the city entrance and takes it up to the top of the hill opposite Hebron. This is the same gate where they were waiting to kill Samson which is just like when Judas came with armed men and betrayed Christ in the Garden.

What is so special about the hill opposite Hebron? Well, there are two patriarchs of old buried at the top of that hill. Their graves have been memorialized so that tourists can still visit this day. One is Jesse, the father of King Beloved (David) and the other is Ruth, the Moabitess who was redeemed by Boaz. The Power of God relocated the door to the harlot (Israel) and took it to the house of David and the redeemed gentile. Coincidence? Do you still believe that story of Samson is about a strong man constantly chasing women of the night? Oh, and Ruth's husband Boaz's name means "In him is strength". Glory! You just can't make this stuff up!

We have evidence of an alternative view that reveals Samson as an appointed Judge representing the Power of God and we haven't yet talked about Delilah. We haven't searched out any Hebrew words. We simply retold the same story with an alternative plot that utilized all the nouns of the story rather than accepting passed down traditions. Traditions that only focused on verses that lead to what the originators of these traditions wanted us to see. Who are the originators of these passed down traditions? I can only speculate.

After seven hours of teaching the Story of Samson, several people in the Sunday School class are crying, including the Pastor's wife. They had never seen the Samson Story as God's effort to reveal His Power. They unanimously agreed they had it wrong the first week of this Story. God is good, He always shows up and reveals Himself. Glory to the King!

Adult Sunday School is a gift. Thank you, Lord.

Honor of Kings

I'm a creationist and very aware of the phrase "intelligent design". So far, we have only performed the *Honor of Kings* for about ten words. We have an entire Bible to get done! Within my first week of studying the Hebrew letters it was as though I was amidst a maze of understanding. Every time I turned a corner there was more revelation. It felt like I was exploring a hiking trail through the DNA helix. It wasn't a brain effort. There is life in each Word. In my past I memorized verses with very little understanding of each word. Now I am learning words that bring life to each verse.

The next two Hebrew words we will research are Stone and Rock (Ms. Mable). I love these two words and I especially love sharing their Hebrew origins together. The word for stone is Abn (אבן) and the Hebrew word for Rock is Tzur (צור).

The Same Story Again The definition of the letters that spell Abn (אבן) is, "God's (א) House (ב) is Life (ן)." What's even more interesting is that the 1ˢᵗ two letters of Stone (אבן) spell Aba (אב) which means Father and the last two letters spell the word Ben (בן) which means Son. The Father and the Son are a stone.

I spent a lot of time meditating on past teaching and scriptures after learning that the Father and the Son are a Stone.

Acts 4:11 KJV: This is the stone (אבן) which was set at nought of you builders, which is become the head of the corner.

They rejected the Father and the Son. Enjoy rewiring all the other stone-related scriptures of your past. What a beautiful 15 seconds!

The Same Story Again The definition of the letters that spell Tzur(צור) is, "Righteousness (צ) is the Straight-up Man with the Nail (ו) and the Prince (ר)." This literally means that Jesus while walking on the Earth and Jesus in Heaven are both representations of Righteousness. Glory to the King!

The Same Story Again Do you see it? A stone (abn אבן) is the Father (aba אב) and the Son (ben בן), and a Rock (tzur צור) is just the Son (ben בן). Again, the Hebrew letters of the word for Rock tell us that the Son was righteous while He walked on earth and while He is a Prince of His Father in Heaven.

The Same Story Again So, He tells Peter that upon this rock (tzur צור) I will build My church. First, know that we will reveal the Hebrew word for church later. But for now, add to this that Peter's father's name is Jonah. Remember, "Simon bar Jonah"?

Matthew 16:17 KJV: And Jesus answered and said unto him, Blessed art thou, Simon ***Barjona***: for flesh and blood hath not revealed it unto thee, but my Father which is in heaven.

Matthew 16:17 NKJV: Jesus answered and said to him, "Blessed are you, Simon ***Bar-Jonah***, for flesh and blood has not revealed this to you, but My Father who is in heaven.

Matthew 16:17 NIV: Jesus replied, "Blessed are you, ***Simon son of Jonah***, for this was not revealed to you by flesh and blood, but by my Father in heaven.

As you can see, the translation of the Greek "Simon Bar Jonah" is different for the KJV, NKJV, and NIV.

Together, the three translations reveal that the word "Bar" is another spelling of the word Son. Sure, most Bible studiers know that Bar means son and they know that "Simon Barjona" means "Simon son of Jonah". I was 10 years old when my Granddad gave me my own KJV Bible for my birthday. I read it from cover-to-cover in a year. I was over 60 years old when I learned Jonah means Dove. I taught children's church in 2022. The adult that taught with me and the kids ages 8-13 learned that Peter's father was named Jonah which means Dove. Glory to the King!

The Hebrew name Jonah means Dove and the son of Dove is the Rock of the Church. Just ponder on that. Can you imagine how Biblical study and revelation would be different if the noun Jonah were translated, and The Book of Jonah was named The Book of Dove? As we continue, we will keep a list of the TRANSLATED names of the books of the Bible.

- Book of Friend (Ruth)
- Book of Dove (Jonah)

How appropriate for Yeshua (ישוע) to build His church on the son of Dove (the symbol of the spirit). Thank you, Father, I love Your Word in Your language!

Glory to the King?

Chapter 7

U-iitzr (וייצר) – Formed

Life

There were times where I believe I witnessed Cowboy's arms fighting his voice for space in the room. He constantly reminds me that he is more than six feet tall and that I am not. (laughing) His family's life story would be a blockbuster movie. I'm not kidding! I will continue to only highjack parts of that story. That said, this book would not have ever been written if we had not met and for no reason that I can explain, adopted me at one of the lowest times of life. For now, know that they have four adopted children but lost one through injustice and all of them are wonderfully crazy different.

I can only estimate that it was around May 2006. I came to work one day, and Bruce proclaims to have never realized that I drive a Toyota Rav4. I know, why does that even matter, right? He claims that the software I am creating for the company depends on me staying alive. He literally tells me, "Dude, if a squirrel runs across the road while you're doing 50 MPH, you could swerve and hit a tree and die in that vehicle. You have got to get a real vehicle so that if you wreck, you live to talk about it."

I search and find this 2001, red, 4-door, jacked-up, F350 in near perfect condition and drive it to work in that same week. I must admit, the 1st time I got behind the wheel of that truck, I thought I was 6'5" tall. For sure, I felt that I was taller than Bruce. Did I mention that Bruce had a 2006, brown, 4-door, jacked-up, F350 King Ranch?

Well, as fate would have it, the very next week, diesel went to $3.50 per gallon. Man, I was hot! It cost me more than $100 dollars to fill up my truck. I sat in the office and Bruce could tell I wasn't happy. He had not seen me this mad in a long time. You know Bruce, Mr. Nobody Can Have a Bad Day. So, with that voice that impacts me like a loud heavy metal radio station, he asked me, "What's wrong dude?"

I replied with passion, "It costs me over $100 dollars to fill up that truck!"

He literally started laughing and I just continued typing software code. Finally, with more passion I said, "I'm buying a motorcycle!"

Now he is really laughing and asked me if I had ever ridden a motorcycle to which I replied that I had not. He is laughing louder and a few minutes later I hear him talking on the phone to his nephew about which motorcycle he would recommend for two old nerds. He hung up the phone and told me to get in his truck and let's go get us a motorcycle. This is life with Bruce. Never a dull moment and the most positive attention I have received in my life.

I can relate to people that don't know or haven't yet experienced loving your neighbor as yourself. Sure, I had always been generous and caring. I knew compassion and empathy but after the pains of my past I was unaware that my eyes were generally looking inward instead of outward. At this time in my life, I was aware that my pains in life were controlling me and hurting all that I love. I am 47 years old, and I am a mess.

Bruce and I arrived at West Side Honda in Houston, and his nephew has already prepared two 2006 KLR650's for us. This bike is tall and my short-legged 5'8" body has to tip-toe to prevent the bike from falling over. Bruce has me drive it in the parking lot so he can analyze how much work he must do to keep me alive. He tells me that most motorcyclist get killed because the other driver didn't see them. So, he goes inside and purchases two of these little orange flags and bolts them to the luggage rack of our bikes. We literally have what looks like the flag from the 16th hole at Augusta extending 4 feet above the back of our bike. Many times, at a red-light a kid in the vehicle next to me would ask what my motorcycle is. I think it reminded them of Disney Land.

So, we go back inside, and we buy our bikes and all the protective gear needed to hopefully survive without road rash in the case of an accident. We throw the bikes in the back of the truck and head home.

Bruce took me on my very first motorcycle riding adventure and IT WAS SO COOL!!! We drove all the way from Alvin to Freeport and back. I witnessed many potential life ending scenarios while following behind him. I had no idea how motorcyclists must be aware of every driver around them.

I spent the night at Bruce's house, and we rode our bikes to work. Wow, what an experience. Our CEO noticed these two green motorcycles with a flag drive through the gate and immediately came down the hall spitting and screaming mad. All he could see was a double funeral. He was hot! I had never witnessed such behavior.

Christian Hebrew Study

It is still March 2022, and our Sunday School class has embraced the Biblical view of the Story of Samson rather than the passed down traditions.

Now it is time to reveal the last woman in the Samson story, Delilah. Delilah is such a conversation piece. First, note that nowhere in the story does it state that Samson married Delilah, nor does it state they ever had sex. It is also cool that Samson's name means Sunshine and Lilah means Nighttime. You can already see that they are not a match.

Delilah means low languishing which hints some undescribed mental state that is below normal. Well, we know that she accepts 1,100 pieces of silver from each of the five lords of the Philistines (Trespassers), so she obviously can negotiate business. She is rich but in Hebrew the number eleven is "One Short". There were 12 tribes in Israel and 12 disciples. Peter led the effort to replace Judas after the crucifixion because there must be 12. The 12th letter of the Hebrew alphabet is the Lamed which means authority, or government. Is it possible that Delilah means low languishing because though she is a business manager, she lacks understanding of the ways God which is why she has no clue of who Samson represents?

Here is a great comparison. How many times was Jesus tempted? The obvious answer is three. Well, that's how many times He was tempted by the devil. He was tempted many times by people requesting Him to come off the cross. Let's categorize the many temptations at the cross as one occurrence. So, Jesus was tempted four times which is the same number of times that Delilah tempted Samson before she got what she wanted.

My study reveals that Delilah represents the world, the beauty used to tempt Christ to bow down and worship. To further prove that she represents the world, research the definition of the original Hebrew names of the five lords of the Philistines that each paid eleven-hundred pieces of silver. The meanings of their Hebrew names represent many of the offices needed to form a government. So, Samson loved Delilah (the world) just like Jesus so loved the world (John 3:16).

There are many more concealed references in the Story of Samson (Sunshine) that expose (Gilgal) he represents the Power of God. Is it fulfilling to know that Samson, whose Hebrew name is Shimshone which means Sunshine, represents the Power of God? Is it also fulfilling to entertain the idea that the same Sun in the sky that the pagan entities aspire to credit to themselves conceals a visible understanding of the Power of God? He is so powerful that He created the Sun with the ability to heat and cool the entire earth. And it does that every day without any sign of its power diminishing. That is power! My Savior, the great creator of all things revealed His power in the story of Shimshone (Samson).

Honor of Kings

There are so many interesting words to research in the creation story. I chose the word translated as "Formed" because it's a quick and simple study that provides wonderful conjecture. The phrase "Let us make man in our image" is a topic of conversation for the ages. Studying Hebrew doesn't NAIL the answer, but it does add a new thread of conjecture. I won't participate in writing books on a single Biblical subject topic, but I do enjoy visiting with those that do. I am addicted to this new form of study.

It's probably a good idea to periodically remind you that I am a Christian and Jesus is my Savior. I believe in the death, burial, and resurrection of the Son of God. Yes, you can learn and study Hebrew without losing the faith in the Gospel. I have far more friends that have left the faith without studying Hebrew than those that have. I have very little tolerance for the religious crowds that voice otherwise and feel at liberty to express their misunderstandings. Ugh! God, bless them for they know not what they say! Oh my, let me stop.

Reviewing the definition of the letters for the word translated as Formed in Genesis 2:7 is a bit different. Visually the first thing I notice about the word is the First and Last letters. They are both letters that represent Jesus. One is the Vav (ו) which is the Straight Up Man with the Nail. And the other is the Resh (ר) which is the Prince or Head. So, Jesus proclaims in the Book of the Revelation that He is the First and the Last and the First and Last letters of the Hebrew word translated as Formed represent Christ. Glory to the King! So, you have Jesus as a man and Jesus resurrected as the Prince, Head of the House on both sides of the remaining three letters (ייצ) in the middle. The three letters in the middle include two Yods (יי). The Yod (י) is the Hand That Does Might Deeds and this word has two Yods (יי) which suggest that whatever God did, it included Him using both hands.

I mentioned earlier that when God created everything during creation week, the words used for creating only had one Yod, or my interpretation is that He used one hand. But to form man he used Both hands. I love that! Is it absolute fact? Well, for me it is. The last letter in the middle is the Tsadi (צ) which is the letter for Righteousness. Well, of course, right?

Now, let me summarize and repeat. The Hebrew word for "Formed" in Genesis 2:7 hints to the idea that it was done by the life of Jesus, The Resurrected Christ, Both Hands of the Father, and their Righteousness. No, I can't make doctrine out of it, but I sure can love it and magnify my Savior and Creator.

The word "Formed" is found in the KJV 31 times. The Hebrew word translated as Formed in Genesis 2:7 is unique, only one time in the Hebrew text. I truly do not have a clue of what God was doing when He formed man, but I am also 100% certain that if we were to witness it, we wouldn't call it "forming". I truly have no idea of how to properly translate this word. I would likely write an entire paragraph explaining what I don't know. My Bible translation would be too big to carry to church. (laughing)

Genesis 2:7 KJV: And the Lord God formed (וייצר) man of the dust of the ground, and breathed into his nostrils the breath of life; and man became a living soul.

Glory to the King!

Chapter 8

Oreb (ערב) – Evening and
Boker (בקר) – Morning

Life

I guess it's time to give an employment update. It's January 2006, and I spent hundreds of hours researching the business operations to gain understanding of exactly how this program is going to be able to automate, measure, and improve operational success and grow net income. It's time to test my findings.

Story goes that one day while sitting at my desk, I turned around and told Bruce, the Chief Technology Officer (CTO), "Dude, we are not managing this business correctly."

Mr. CTO, a man I have never met because I never pushed that button, shows himself and is now required to deal with my flagrant arrogance. With his new corporate intercom voice he replies, "These guys have built this business and have been running it for years. How in the world can you justify such a comment? Go ahead dude, tell me what you would do differently."

That's how revelation works. You could share time with someone every day for seven months and they are still blind to exactly what you are doing. I am automating our operation. I already have operational measurements that lead me to understanding employee behavior that can be measured that will result in more efficient and profitable operational success. I did all this work, this huge investment of hours, while working in the same office, yet even he doesn't realize that automating business operations provides keen insight into the best way for it to be done, especially if you are a freak of research like me.

I had witnessed night crews sleeping and not servicing an aircraft that just pulled up on the ramp. Literally, the pilot realizes that even his jet engines didn't wake this guy up. I witnessed evening crews using corporate supplies to wax their own cars. I witnessed that it is normal human behavior to perform slightly below the commitment inspected. Hence, if there is zero inspection then the job performance standard is far below standard.

We do not perform at the same standard after 10pm that we perform at 10am. We know it and we intentionally ignore it. We lie. We hire a new employee and tell them that they are going to be a Line Service Professional and then as quickly as possible we put them working on the 10pm – 6am shift where there are seldom any aircraft. Then we complain when the building janitorial services are not done by the overnight shift. They aren't Line Service Professionals; they are glorified custodians. Of course, we talked for at least an hour.

It was obvious that Bruce understood and knew my view of the problem and how to fix it would be good for the company. He realized my comment wasn't arrogance nor was it "smoke and mirrors". I could see Bruce's wheels turning and he asked, "Could you do this behind the scenes? Can you do all that you talked about without anyone knowing or being required to give permission?"

I replied, "Yes, I can, and I will set up a test run for the following month, February 2006."

Well, here goes Mr. Over Passionate. I decided to give the effort a name. I called it Rooster. It was my way of signaling a wake-up call to reveal methods of operation not yet implemented. I want so badly to provide the details of the test run but that is for another book (maybe). Let's just say it truly renovated how to operate and manage the Aviation FBO Industry.

Well, surprise! My efforts and process changes were not well received. I still believe it is because of my over-passionate personality that most people love to hate. My personal career took quite a downturn and my immature method of introducing the program received its just reward. The name Rooster was taken as an insult. To this day it's a well-known word and the ultimate insult to the founder of the company. However, nobody was bold enough to express that displeasure until the middle of the month of February. That said, I recognized that Rooster was about to get undermined and shut down, so I taught the team how to carry on without me until the end of the month.

In those days it took the accounting team about three months before financials were published. Later I automated the financial reporting process so the time to produce financial reporting was reduced to 15-20 days. The story goes that Bruce was sitting in the monthly management meeting next to the CEO who slid him a note showing that February was one of the most profitable months in our company's history. Rooster was a financial success!

Well, from what I was told, my brother's defensive nature kicked in and the meeting experienced quite a disruption when the speaking mechanical bull began flinging his arms. It would be 10 years before the company would break the production records of Rooster, February 2006, yet the methods of Rooster would never be requested, defined, shared, adopted, or implemented as an operational standard.

Many years later (2019) I did it again. Somehow, I won the favor of the GM at our White Plains (HPN) facility. During her initial employment training I confidentially told her about Rooster and after a few months on the job she contacted me and wanted Rooster implemented. She is an amazing leader and wanted her team to embrace this training.

We trained every employee on these processes that were renamed "Moneyball". Moneyball was implemented behind the scenes and these operational processes were uninterrupted for three years. Once again, the success was breaking corporate records nearly every month, but because it was done without permission, the executive management team innocently hijacked the success measurements claiming the results were from their efforts. Efforts that were not duplicated at any of our other twelve locations.

In February 2023, new corporate operational standards eliminated our ability to continue Moneyball. Nonetheless, it took a couple months before those decisions impacted the customer so 2023 Qtr #1 was still a business record. The business dropped rapidly starting in April.

Are you curious about what was "Moneyball"? Well, it is actually very simple. If it was difficult then you couldn't do it behind the scenes. Moneyball is our best effort to implement technology in our business similar to my perception of how the movie Moneyball impacted Baseball. Well, people in our business that watch the show would still struggle understanding what I am talking about. Why? Well because likely nobody in the FBO Industry has ever managed the entire data environment required to operate an FBO. It is far more complex than baseball which proves it is far more necessary. Add to that, everybody enjoys being measured to prove they are on a winning streak or to prove they are better today than yesterday. That said, we devised methods of measuring success. No, not stupid stuff that would be unappealing but rather we found the equivalent of our batting average, home runs, wins, and losses. Basically, if we couldn't measure it, then we didn't do it. A successful team loves watching their stats!

Christian Hebrew Study

It's now April 2022 and the church has given permission for our **Saturday** Bible study group to meet at the church fellowship hall. Wow! The whole gang shows up as well as a few church members that were interested to see what this Saturday Bible Study is all about. The worship team cranks it up.

The Pastor was in his office preparing for the next day's sermon and could hear us, so he comes to the door of the fellowship hall and simply stands there and worships with us. It is obvious that he is proud to have us there and amazed by the talents of the worship team. God is good! A few days later, Pastor told me that he needed that worship time.

I hope you are as excited as me to learn what was the next subject shared in our Adult Sunday School class. Yes, I always did my marketing during class so that everyone knew what was next. Well, one of God's Appointed times known as Passover had just passed so I scheduled to begin teaching what the Bible teaches about God's Appointed Times. In the original Hebrew scriptures, it's called "Moedim".

One of the most misunderstood references to Passover is that it is a Jewish holiday. Sure, the Jews celebrate Passover, but Passover existed long before the Jews did. The first mention of Moedim (מועדים) - God's Appointed Times is the 4th Day of Creation. This was another seven-week class that, like Samson, introduced more confrontations of how passed down traditions contradicted Biblical text.

Honor of Kings

The creation story of Genesis is one of the best known and most retold of all Biblical stories. There are so many options of words to choose from. Words that make us rethink how we view the creation story. I am sure that we will review many of those as this book series continues. For this initial publication, I have chosen the Hebrew words for Evening and Morning. For me, they have a beautiful hidden message that will once again demonstrate the power and beauty of "living by every word that proceedeth…" By now, you know the routine. Let's review the definitions of the words translated as evening and morning from the Hebrew letters that spell these words.

My definition of Oreb (Evening ערב) from the Hebrew letters is, "See (ע) the Prince (ר) return to His house (ב)." Isn't that cool? The definition of evening insinuates we are watching the light return to its house. What is more special is that the Hebrew letter Resh (ר) can mean either prince or head. That said, the letter and the paleo Hebrew pictograph always show the head facing away from the direction that Hebrew is read which would be sunset. It is also awesome to see that the last letter of the word is the Bet (ב) which means house and for me it is as though the sunset is us watching the Prince turn off the lights of His house. I LOVE IT! I can already guess what morning is going to be.

The definition of Boker (Morning בקר) from the Hebrew letters is, "The Holy (ק) Prince (ר) leaves His house (ב). Again, as mentioned many times, anybody that learns Hebrew is granted the privilege to derive these definitions from their own understanding of the definition of the letters. Many people see these definitions differently than me, but all the definitions bring glory to the depth of meaning of this Holy language. A language I believe to be the heavenly language and the language created by our creator. The language that defines The Word. Simple and beautiful.

Isn't it great to believe in the Son of God. To learn that His language tells us all about Him. Though I love re-learning my Bible while including these 15-second additions. I know that my salvation is not based on me passing a final exam when I am called up yonder. But what I do know is that my strength, faith, and ability to conquer temptation is greatly enhanced as my knowledge grows. The more I know about Him the better I know Him. I think that is normal and to be expected. It just happens. It's not a brain thing.

Glory to the King!

Chapter 9

Kphr (כפר) – Atonement

Life

What a difference a day makes! A couple months after we arrived from Cincinnati, we rolled out the 1st version of the program to just one of our locations for testing. It was the summer of 2006, and the company was kind enough to allow my daughter to do a college internship. Little did I know she would witness the highlight of my career.

My daughter was allowed to sit in the monthly meeting with the owners of our franchisees and the corporate management team. Bruce, the CTO, also attends the meeting each month. I never attend meetings. Well, the story goes that I was sitting at my desk and Bruce returns from the meeting and the room can barely contain his presence. Somebody put a microphone on the volume knob and his passion was overflowing. He was pumped! Oh wait, I just noticed my daughter standing behind one of his flapping wings. (laughing)

Bruce says, "Dude, I didn't know it but during this week's conference call they asked the owner using your software how well it was working. Then Bruce attempts to mimic the owner's slow and distinct voice as he repeats his words, "That it's not a good program. (pause) It's not a great program. (pause) IT'S A REVOLUTIONARY PROGRAM. The software is going to change how the entire industry utilizes technology."

I can't possibly express how it felt that day. Not only was the program going to be implemented throughout the organization, but it was such a gift for my daughter to be in attendance in that meeting when this news was shared. Vindication, sweet vindication. It could have all ended in Cincinnati. There was evening and then there was morning, and then the software was invented. (Smile)

Bruce and I successfully rolled out an enterprise software program in one year. For the technology folks it was an ERP Client Server Program. I was a bit surprised that there wasn't any form of compensation for a job well done. My first-year anniversary passed and there wasn't a performance appraisal or pay increase. I am not the type of person that will ever ask. I'm not going to elaborate on any conversations about compensation. Bottom line is after the first year, after working far more than 3,000 hours there was no acknowledgment. I love my co-workers and I love the job. Life is different. I will just continue and see how it goes.

I intentionally did not share my daughter's name in this story. Years after this amazing personal event we had a disagreement, and we haven't spoken since a conversation the night before my mother's funeral in March 2011. She and her husband chose not to attend the funeral. At the time of this writing, it has been thirteen years. Her sister Anna and I talk regularly. Kids have no idea how their voice and their presence play such a healing role in life. This silence leaves a void that is seldom out of vision. That said, I feel that I am truly reaping what I sowed. I went nearly ten years suffering in bitterness and not sharing life with my parents. God has forgiven me and now I pray for His grace and mercy and not require my sweet daughter to experience what I have gone through. God says to honor your mother and father that our days be long on the earth. I learned the worse way possible that He did not say they had to deserve it.

Christian Hebrew Study

It's still April 2022. My timing might be off a month or two, but the Community Church voted me as Vice-Trustee. It's a privilege though it's merely a legalistic position assisting with the responsibility of maintaining the church. I'm new to this community. It's a gift to be included.

It was also approximately this time when the Church announced the beginning efforts to disassociate from the United Methodist Church. There were obvious good reasons. Several good men are working diligently to get this accomplished. It was necessary but at the end of the day, it's business, church business. Is "Church Business" an oxymoron? To propose the question proves I don't need the sermon. (laughing)

Sunday School is enjoying the Study of the Moedim – God's Appointed Times. There are literally dates on the Calendar that God has set for His Appointed Times. Just as the USA Government has written certain dates of the yearly calendar as Holidays, God has written certain dates of the calendar as Holy Days. Is the enunciation and spelling of the words Holy Days and Holidays simply a coincidence? One can only wonder. It should not be a surprise to learn that all the dates on both calendars have a history. We can research the origin and history of each USA holiday becoming law as well as learning the origin of any of God's Holy Days in scripture.

This book includes three simultaneously developing stories for the purpose of entertaining the reader so that it isn't a 100% teaching book. Almost nobody has ever re-read their college History 101 book for pleasure. I am near 100% certain that a fraction of inspired book readers would tolerate a complete book of me teaching on every page. I can't even fathom the thought of compiling such text. Ok, so what are we going to do? I want to share fundamental information available on the internet, but I don't want a long bibliography section acknowledging other works. I got it. I will just talk about what I have learned in my past and allow you the freedom to research and validate for yourself. Until you do so, then everything I am declaring is conjecture. I am 100% good with that. Let's begin.

The origin of God's Holy days is found in the Book of Leviticus. There is scriptural proof that these dates existed prior to Moses coming down from Mt Sinai but bottom line is that they all existed long before our government's passing of holidays by law. Our governing calendar is called The Gregorian Calendar, and it is based on the schedule of the Sun. God's Moedim are scheduled off a lunar schedule. Very few of these dates fall on the same date of the calendar.

There are three most common Holy Days and holidays for the same purpose. Both God's Appointed Times and our country's holidays celebrate the Birth, Death, and Resurrection of our Savior Jesus Christ. Yes, they do not recognize His birthday as the same date on the calendar. The name of the holiday that celebrates His birth is Christmas and the name of the Holy Day that celebrates His birth is called Sukkot. Christmas falls on December 25th of each year while depending on the lunar schedule Sukkot generally falls in late September but sometimes in early October.

Christmas along with several other holidays became law in 1870. That is correct, initially our founding fathers did not legalize Christmas which was already a holiday in their countries of origin. It appears that freedom of religion was synonymous with not having to acknowledge Christmas. One of the arguments I have studied about scheduling Christ's Birthday on December 25th was so that it would be acknowledged as a viable religion because all the other worshippers of other religions used this date as a celebration. I won't elaborate.

Few Christians are aware that Jesus's Birthday is provided to us in the New Testament. I always knew that December 25th wasn't Jesus's actual birthday. That date was established before I was born and most everyone is aware that it's to celebrate the occasion but it's not His actual birthday. That said, what changes when we learn about His birthday? Is it okay to behave differently? Is it okay to share? Is it okay to share in church?

Jesus's Birthday is concealed in the New Testament scriptures, nonetheless, it is there! Let's search it out!

We know from Mary's visit with Elizabeth, the mother of John the Baptist, that Jesus is six months younger than John (Luke 1:36). So, if we know John's birthday then we know Jesus's Birthday. We learn that John's father is a priest of the division of Abia (Abijah in the Old Testament). The Old Testament reveals that his division served in the temple the week before Shavuot, the feast of the Wheat Harvest. It's also the custom that all priests serve on the Appointed Times, se he served the following week during Shavuot as well. He returned home, and 40 weeks later John was born. That would schedule Elizabeth's due date during the week of Passover. Because this is a God appointed birth, I believe John was born on Passover, the 15th Day of the month Nissan. Jesus would be six months later, the 15th Day of the month Tishri which is also the 1st Day of Sukkot also called the Feast of Tabernacles or The Feast of Booths. On our Gregorian calendar the 15th of Tishri is usually late September.

I can only wonder if this knowledge was more common during the conservative and formative years that our country was founded. Did this knowledge play a role in explaining why it took nearly 100 years before these holidays became law? It's just conjecture, what do you think? Again, this is easy to search out.

Honor of Kings

It is such a treat to share the *Honor of Kings* effort to reveal hidden revelations about the Hebrew word Kphr (כפר - pronounced Kafar) that is translated as Atonement. The definition of the word from the Hebrew letters is, "The hand that holds (כ) the words (פ) of the Prince (ר)."

There are many revelations to be gleaned. The word Atonement is in the KJV 70 times, 69 times in the Old Testament and only once in the New Testament. I know, I was shocked to learn that as well. There are many Hebrew words that are translated as Atonement. A couple of those Hebrew words translated as Atonement are in scripture one time. What do we do with those stats? Once again, we have Hebrew words in scripture one time that are not translated as a unique English word. We are talking about the word Atonement!

I have heard hundreds of sermons about atonement. It is one of the most preached topics and most repeated words throughout the history of preachers. But from my recollection it is seldom referenced in sermons from Old Testament scriptures. I am truly struggling remembering one time that atonement was mentioned in a sermon that it does not reference a New Testament foundation. Hilarious, from all the sermons I have heard I would have "bet the farm" that the word atonement was in the New Testament far more times than the old.

Exodus 29:36 KJV: And thou shalt offer every day a bullock for a sin offering for <u>atonement</u> (הכפרים): and thou shalt cleanse the altar, when thou hast made an <u>atonement</u> (בכפרך) for it, and thou shalt anoint it, to sanctify it.

Since learning Hebrew, I love this verse for FAR DIFFERENT reasons. It has the word atonement in the verse twice and both of the Hebrew spellings have prefix and suffix letters added to the noun so that neither is spelled identical to the three letters that spell the word Kphr כפר. As you can see, the root Hebrew noun (כפר) for atonement is underlined within each word but nonetheless, the words are different yet translated identical. Earlier we showed that the plural form of a Hebrew word has the Hebrew letters Yod-Mem (ים) at the end of the word. So, you can also see that one of the Hebrew words is plural, yet the translation is singular.

The Same Story Again I am determined not to render this book as an analytical view of scripture. Hence, I refrained from continuing the documentation of the *Honor of Kings* efforts provided in Chapter 1. During a Bible study in September 2023, I provided an Excel spreadsheet on the use of the word Atonement in both the original Hebrew text and English from the KJV. I found that many of the same Hebrew words that were translated as atonement are many times translated as something other than atonement. I also ***estimate*** that if you researched each of the Hebrew words that were translated as atonement in the English translations that there would be approximately 150-200 instances of those Hebrew words in the Tanakh (Old Testament) yet they were only translated as Atonement 70 times. Undoubtedly, doing the *Honor or Kings* search on this matter would reveal multiple instances of revelation worthy of sharing.

First, let me rest your mind and confirm that the Hebrew research reveals that Atonement is a covering (more precise would be a propitiatory shelter). I believe that to be very consistent with what I was taught in church and hopefully you agree. My struggle continuing to reveal the *Honor of Kings* effort is that this is a doctrine-based word so any hint of variation from fundamental doctrine is not going to be received well. That said, I can reveal that approximately 100 times in the English translations of the Old Testament, the same Hebrew words that are translated as Atonement are translated as something other than Atonement. Anyone can do the *Honor of Kings* and search out these instances of a covering that are not revealed, discussed, or taught as a form of a covering.

People are okay declaring these facts for a lesser important word but not for Atonement. Declaring the same to be true for the word Purification would not be nearly as bothersome. Purification is not embedded into the bedrock of the Church doctrines like the word Atonement.

Okay then, so what does all this mean? It means I must stay true to my purpose. My purpose is not to enter conflict with any church or church doctrine by providing my personal opinions of revelation from these efforts. I will simply reveal what I have searched out from the *Honor of Kings* efforts and allow each person to read, confirm as desired, and apply the newly found knowledge as they are led. I can't even tell my kids what to do, but I can show them why I did what they witnessed. Why the change? What did I learn that led to these decisions? Just FYI – It doesn't change salvation but it does bring more understanding of common topics.

Chapter 10

Thulduth (תולדות) – Generation

Life

I began my software engineering career in the early '80's after the desktop PC became available. Well, obviously, any software used in those days falls under the category of legacy which means it has been superseded by modern technology. That's one of the problems with technology, even to this day. Once a programmer or software company develops a successful product, the available technologies change and the entire product becomes legacy and now the cost to maintain existing while improving to current technologies is far more expensive and many times unsuccessful. I have personally witnessed large corporations spend millions attempting to convert well written legacy (old) technology into modern technologies and at the end of the day, the result is total failure and money wasted.

If you think working with technology has a legacy issue, can you imagine working with a modern-day John Wayne? The only difference I see between Bruce and John Wayne is that Bruce doesn't use the word "Pilgrim". He is as legacy as they come. I guess if we live long enough, we will find some form of legacy all around us. That said, once you notice it and acknowledge its existence, it seems to be screaming foundational messages that are soon to be lost. Messages that if lost will result in some form of deficit. That is especially true with Bruce.

One of Bruce's legacies is that he does not tolerate anybody telling lies. We work in the technology field. In our company, Bruce and I are the entire technical staff. He is the Network Engineer, and I am the Software Engineer. We both wear cowboy hats to work (I started wearing my cowboy hat to work not long after meeting Bruce), we both drive F350 trucks, we both ride green KLR650 motorcycles, and we share the same office. People at work are starting to call me mini-Bruce.

Anyways, back to him being "legacy". So, you think legacy is the same as "old fashioned". No, this is very different. Old-fashioned is related to your clothes, music you desire, or even giving opinions that you know before you speak that they are from the past. Legacy is when all of that is just who you are 100% of the time and it is never an act or a show. I work for a long-haired man that looks like Willie Nelson but aspires to be John Wayne. The is my brother! Yes, he has faults, but you will have to find those out from somebody besides me.

Honor of Kings

The efforts of the *Honor of Kings* will unveil beautiful revelation about the Hebrew spelling of the First time the word "Generation" is used in scripture. We will see that the spelling of the word changes after the fall of man and we will reveal the amazing story that God choses to reestablish the original spelling of the word which is also the Last time the original spelling appears in scripture. Have you noticed the continual "First and the Last" references in the research? Enjoy as we take a walk down Bible legacy and once again search out what He has concealed within the *Honor of Kings* of the word Generations. But first, let's take a snapshot view of what libraries of books share about the legacy of the Canon.

Christian Hebrew Study

There are thousands of people employed to manage corporate documents. These documents are called "Controlled Documents" and used to manage complex industrial processes, repairing a specific manufacturer and model of aircraft, etc. The key is that there is a single document for each purpose. If there is a need for a change to the document, then there is a document that provides a procedure that must be followed to implement a change. This "Controlled Documents" process even includes the versioning of each document so that the history of all changes is documented.

Yes, I could continue elaborating on this very common workflow in many industries. Can you imagine the impact of our world if that process were implemented on the Holy Scriptures. Can you imagine having one divine and inspired English translation that also includes a book that provides all approved historical changes to the Holy Scriptures with explanations of the change. I can't imagine there would ever be a formation of an organization that would undertake the effort to document the history of all English translations.

There are now approximately one hundred English translation with the words "Holy Bible" on the cover and available for purchase to your children and mine with no control or approval of content. I have not researched but it seems that all these translations have been accepted by the church and by omission of disapproval they are deemed divine and inspired. I have witnessed videos of preachers endorsing a particular translation and claiming the accuracy should be used to correct the original Greek or Hebrew text.

While learning Hebrew, it is impossible not to become aware of the legacy of what we call "The Canon". I personally found it impossible to not become passionately aware of the Septuagint, and other books that have been either removed from the Canon, deemed to no longer be divine and inspired, or both. Many of us are aware of these books. The Book of Enoch, Book of Jubilees, Wisdom of Solomon, and a few books that are still included in the Septuagint but no longer in the Canon. All these books are considered inspired and divine in many Bibles of various countries throughout the world. That's right, the Books included and excluded from the KJV vary from one country and/or continent to the next. Why? Well, I can only conclude it is because of the entity that decides these things, the Catholic Church.

Can you imagine living in 1684 when a list of books of the Bible were removed and deemed no longer the divine and inspired Word of God? Yes, there is crazy legacy and history that rest on dusty shelves that hide the history of activities that would incite religious riots today. The modern way to achieve these changes in our society is the introduction of new Bible translations that provide acceptance and tolerance to actions profoundly declared as sin in our past. We now have drag queens ordained as Godly ministers. In some countries there are people serving prison sentences for verbally declaring their opposition to these translations. Unlike 1684, no book of the Bible had to be removed to establish sinful activities as modern-day righteous alternatives of Godly living. Instead, new translations are introduced and immediately upon publication inherit divine and inspired authorship equal to any other version. Or, by simply changing the course outline of a seminary course, doctrines contrary to our past can become the latest foundations and redefine righteous culture.

Again, by default, studying Hebrew requires all understanding to pass through a narrow pass. Eshtaol (אשתאל) is the Hebrew word translated as "A narrow pass". The root Hebrew Word for Narrow Pass is only spoken twice by our Creator in the original Hebrew text, and both are in the story of Samson, Coincidence?

I am grateful for the English translations, especially the first effort, the KJV. That said, I have also researched the impact of men upon its content. Jesus experienced the same problem. Before Jesus arrives to the scene, the many generations since the law was provided on stones had already rewritten and enforced their own laws on the people.

Making new translations is a method that began before the cross. One example is when He was approached by those that supposedly represent His law and asked Him why His disciples break the traditions of the elders and not wash their hands before they eat. Nothing in God's law says you must do so, thus proving that the laws of God had already become legacy. A way other than His way has replaced His way.

Hebrew study isn't required to expose these stories, it simply helps them become more visible. It is going to be so wonderful when Christians learn how easy it is to learn God's language. The alternative is humorous. I am amused when I hear people say that their Bible is different than the Catholic Bible. Think about it, is there a Bible that has not been somehow influenced by Catholic origin.

One of the character traits adopted by those that study the original Hebrew text is you become very aware of the generations of the divine word, meaning that we know without a doubt that it has been tampered with. I cannot wait for archeologists to find the arc of the covenant and hopefully provide us with the original writings on stone. What a day that will be. Is there evidence in the KJV that the law existed on scrolls before it was written on stone at Mt Sinai?

Well, if you didn't throw this book out the window, then let's search out the hidden treasures, the legacy of the Hebrew words translated as generation or generations. Glory to the King!

Honor of Kings

The first time that the word generations is used in scripture is before the fall of man in Genesis 2:4 which provides the generations of the heavens and the earth when they were created. I won't even attempt to provide conjecture on that topic. The key point here is to review the spelling of the Hebrew word translated as Generations. This spelling of the word only occurs in scripture twice!

Genesis 2:4 KJV: These are the generations (תולדות) of the heavens and of the earth when they were created, in the day that the LORD God made the earth and the heavens,

The next occurrence of the word generations is after the fall of man in Genesis 5:1 and it is providing the generations of Adam after the fall. This use of generations is more common to us. Again, the key point here is to review the spelling of the Hebrew word translated as Generations.

Genesis 5:1 KJV: This is the book (ספר) of the generations (תולדת) of Adam. In the day that God created man, in the likeness of God made he him;

The Same Story Again Note that the Hebrew word for Book is Sphr which means scroll. Ok, so let's zoom in on the spelling of these two Hebrew words and see what's different.

Genesis 2:4 תולדֹוֹת

Genesis 5:1 תולדת

I have underlined the letter in the Genesis 2:4 verse that is not in the Genesis 5:1 verse. That Hebrew letter is the Vav (ו) which represents the Straight Up Man with the Nail. You can see from the letters definition that it provides clear understanding that it represents Christ on the Cross, our redeemer. So, after the fall, the 2nd Vav is removed from the spelling of the word. The spelling in Genesis 5:1 is found seven times in scripture. Seven is the number for perfection. Coincidence?

The Hebrew word in Genesis 2:4 is only found twice in scripture. The other occurrence is in Ruth 4:18.

Ruth 4:18 KJV: Now these are the generations (תולדות) of Pharez: Pharez begat Hezron,

There are many revelations but the first to be shared is that the redeemer letter is reestablished in the word that is only used here and in Genesis 2:4 which is before the fall of man. There are seven spellings of this word without the redeemer letter located between the two spellings.

Is it satisfying to find that the redeemer letter is reestablished in the Book of Ruth (Friend) after she has been redeemed by Boaz?

Is there any revelation hidden in the fact that Pharez is a bastard son from his mother's father-in-law.

Is there any revelation knowing that his mother Tamar is the granddaughter of Shem? Or that she is the daughter of a priest?

Is there any revelation that the law requires that no son of a bastard can be King of Israel until the 10th generation and the 10th generation from Pharez is King Beloved (David)? Glory to the King!

Chapter 11

Thbth (אזוב) – Hyssop

Life

It's football season 2006. That 1st year of work was a blur, and I could write a book about my professional experiences. There were many visits to Bruce's house and the boys are already calling me Uncle Mark. My siblings and I rarely visit so being called Uncle Mark was new to my ears. Impossible to explain why or how, it simply added yet another layer of fondness to this experience.

Still, while work is 60-70 hours a week and still working most weekends, it's all about the boys playing JV football on Thursday evenings, and then we all go to Texas Friday Night Lights. It's Texas-6A varsity football, the largest high schools in Texas are in the 6A classification. Stadiums are huge and the fields are artificial grass, and there isn't an empty seat. Only in Texas! It might be the first time in my life when work consumed most of my week but was not my #1 passion.

Many times, while in the office, Bruce and I would talk about football all week until game day. We talked about last week's game and what the boys did right or wrong. For sure, we would talk about how we would coach them differently but that's what every Texas High School football fan does. Then we would take off work early to go watch practice each day until game day. And then the whole family has dinner together. This is our schedule for ten weeks during football season.

The boys have a few teammates that join us. The 1st one to show up on the scene was Link. Link latched on to us, so he became part of our schedule. It's work, football, church, and food. And Brenda is riding shotgun everywhere. She isn't sitting home by herself, she is cheering, laughing, and participating. She didn't miss any of it. She once said, "You can tell how much of a Christian someone is by how quickly friends become family". Watching her, it seemed to be instantaneous. I literally watch her meet someone and then you see them sitting across the table and eating with us. Sharing life with us means you get a seat at the table. Come eat! She adopted Link at first sight. Now, there are six of us going everywhere together including church. Yep, if you eat with us then you must go to church with us.

I quickly learned that life is all about food. I remember the first time I went to church with them. In the past, Sunday was the only day of the week that

Bruce and I weren't consistently sharing life together. You guessed it, Sunday became another ritual. We work together, we live life after work together, and now we go to church together. Did I mention there was a lot of eating. And there was a lot of eating out. We didn't burden Brenda with hurrying home and cooking. It was football, food, church, and work.

Life with Bruce and his family is clean, virtuous, unselfish, generous, and there are many other character traits that I had never seen within a family. I tried to make sure that I didn't show up at the property before everyone awoke, but nonetheless, when I got there Brenda was quickly at the stove making me breakfast. We would sit on the "King Ranch" porch and talk football until gameday came on TV, and it's more football and more food.

I'm writing, but everyone that has witnessed these stories knows that Bruce is the storyteller. The man can tell a story. The King Ranch porch is one story that requires physical attendance. Impossible to feel the spirit of the story without sitting in that cowboy's presence. While building his house, his brother who is a master carpenter, decides on a design of the wrap-around porch that requires some specialized wood cutting machinery. From what I understand, it's a tool that is used to build custom mansion homes. You have got to see this porch. The ceiling joist beams that support the exposed lumber ceiling are 6"x8" rough cedar with custom curves and they rest on cedar cross beams which are supported by 6"x6" cedar columns. Can you see it? It's stained a dark brown and is strong enough to hold ANYTHING YOU CAN IMAGINE. This is the King Ranch porch that was designed and built without Bruce's approval. Bruce named it the King Ranch porch because it costs more than his King Ranch truck.

Though Bruce is a great storyteller, I also learned that he has a virtue about him. After a year of friendship, I never heard the man say anything that he didn't mean. While witnessing this loud way of walking through life, I also witnessed him to be a man filled to the brim with integrity. It's also impossible not to know the role that Brenda plays in keeping that alive and well. It's unique, beautifully unique.

Football season ends. What's next? It's time for some 6A Texas High School JV basketball. James and Link both decide to play freshman basketball. James is now about six feet tall, and he is just a barrel-chested moose. I remember one night he was running down on defense to prevent a fast break and the opposing player cut in front of him for a layup. The collision looked violent. We know James. We learned that his 200 pounds of solid muscle doesn't have breaks. It looked like a truck smashing a smart car into the wall.

After the game we were eating out (of course), and James made a comment about how they didn't let him play after that incident. Bruce and I laughed, and Bruce said, "Dude, they ejected you from the game. They ruled that was a flagrant foul, thinking you did it on purpose". To know James is to know that he doesn't have a flagrant bone in his body. He did not know he had been ejected. That truck doesn't have brakes.

It's my new family and we are having fun. During games, Brenda is over to one side of me doing her cheers for her boys. During meals, she sits with us at the table while we are loud and crazy. Bruce is loud, I am loud, and Link is loud. James is the opposite of his dad; his volume knob is broken just barely above mumbling. Jacob might be the only normal one. It's craziness and all you can hear is Brenda laughing every minute at every comment made. Everywhere we go is our man-cave. And I can't count how many times a day we all heard Brenda say, "Have I told everybody how much I love y'all today?" or "Glory to the King!"

Christian Hebrew Study

The Saturday Bible study is twice a month on the first and third Saturday of the month. We usually have 25-40 people attend. We start at 10:00am and visit while sharing pot lunch finger food. Then the program starts with worship time and afterwards someone leads the group as we study that week's Torah Portion. Yes, I used the word Torah.

Oh, oh, all my life I was subliminally taught that people that studied the Torah are Jewish and don't believe in Christ but rather they believe in the law and salvation by works. Well, allow me to introduce a new Christian way of life. We are Christians that are Torah Observant and many of us, like me, are devoted researchers of the original Hebrew text. We believe in the Gospel of Jesus, the death, burial, and resurrection of the Son of God. We believe in the New Testament as well as the Old. We believe the Old is the New concealed and the New is the Old revealed. Personally, I spend hours every day researching and learning the original Hebrew text. Is that enough to relax any judgments of using Hebrew words. Later I will provide detail of just what is Torah. It's nothing like I perceived it to be.

I have been meeting with this amazing group of folks for more than two years. Our Saturday study is a voluntary participation, and we simply take an offering to cover the cost of renting the venue each month. If you show up, have your Bible thumping skills ready, these people know their Bible. I cannot remember the last time I attended and didn't learn something new and significant. We ask and answer the most difficult questions without rhetoric or conjecture. Nothing is off-limits and it's okay to get the answer wrong. It's okay to have wonderful discussion for an hour and leave agreeing to disagree.

The group is very complimentary and kind to me. They respect and appreciate those that do the *Honor of Kings*. For me, now that I know how to read and research the Hebrew text, I have questions and I want answers. We answer the most difficult questions. Questions people would never think of asking. That's Torah Fellowship.

Honor of Kings

Earlier while studying the word Donkey, I declared we would search out the Hebrew Word translated as Hyssop used in John 19:29. Well, it's time.

I have a Pastor friend that met my wife and I for a weekend in the Smoky Mountains in late October of 2023 while the Fall leaves were changing colors. He is not a Torah Observant Christian but an awesome friend that doesn't require me to measure my words and has never judged me even though he knows I read and research the Hebrew text. I had prepared him for our visit by letting him know that since we didn't have much time I was going to speed teach three stories of scripture that the church never talks about; 1) What does the water represent when they pierced Jesus side 2) What scripture did Jesus fulfill when he said, "I thirst" in John 19:28-29 and 3) Why did Jesus tell them, "Depart from me, I don't know you."

My friend has an amazing spirit of humility and confessed he had no answer for those three topics and like all other pastor's, he stays away from those topics. Don't we all love honesty and humility. This book will answer all but Question #3. I intend to devote many chapters of *The Same Story Again - Part 2* to answering Question #3.

The definition of Hyssop (אזוב) from the Hebrew letters is another of those that has a visual revelation. The first and last letters of the word Hyssop spells father (abba אב) which is also God's (א) House (ב). The middle two letters are Zayin-Vav (זו) which means the Perfection (ז) of the Straight Up Man with the Nail (ו). So, the definition of Hyssop from the letters is, "The Perfect Straight Up Man with the Nail is inside the House of God, His Father." BEAUTIFUL!!!

Earlier, in Chapter 3 we searched out the Word Cedar. Remember, the definition of the Hebrew letters that spell Cedar is, "The Father (א) and His Son (ר) are Perfect (ז)."

We have almost all the pieces to put this puzzle together and reveal the answers to Questions #1 and #2. Let's add another piece to the puzzle.

John 2:6 NKJV: Now there were set there six waterpots of stone, according to the manner of **purification** of the Jews, containing twenty or thirty gallons

In John 2:6 we see that the pots that were used for His first miracle to turn the water into wine were used for purification. These pots were used to hold purification water. What is purification water? Numbers 19 provides all the details pertaining to the laws of purification. That said, let's look at verse 19:6 to see the list of what is in purification water.

Numbers 19:6 NKJV: And the priest shall take *cedar* wood and *hyssop* and *scarlet*, and cast them into the midst of the fire burning the *heifer*.

Numbers 19:6 shows that there are four components mixed into the water to make purification water. We have already searched out Cedar and we just reviewed Hyssop. Ok, look at the cross one more time. You surely can see His blood which is scarlet. I am betting He was nailed to Cedar wood. And now it says that to fulfill scripture He says that He is thirsty. They use Hyssop to put the drink to His lips.

It seems to me that the scriptures make us focus on the drink. The various translations have us focusing on whether it is water or sour wine, but I believe it is all about the Hyssop. That was the last piece of the puzzle. What's missing? Oh, you think it's the heifer? Well, once the Hyssop touched His lips, He gave up His spirit. Later they pierced His side and not only did blood flow out of His body, but water as well.

If this is the first time you have heard this explanation, then look at that cross one more time. We have been taught all our church days that He is the *Lamb* of God. The blood of the lamb is a covering (atonement) **<u>for our sins</u>**. That is 100% correct! The waters of purification are to **<u>purify us from death</u>**. Purification is not a common topic in church. I would like to introduce the idea that the water that poured out when He was pierced is from His role as the *Heifer* that purifies us from death. He is the Lamb that took away our sin and the Heifer that purifies us from death. This is what Paul speaks of when he refers to the Law of Sin and Death.

Remember the story of the Exodus from Egypt. I won't retell the story, but they put blood over their doorpost. They used Hyssop to dip into the blood. There are two animals on that cross. A lamb for atonement and a heifer for purification.

Glory to the King!

Chapter 12

Ethbe (התבה), Thbth (תבת) – Ark

Life

February 20, 2007, and life is about to undergo another big change. By now, you have probably figured out I'm not married. My second marriage did not survive the abrupt changes of life after the miraculous brain hemorrhage healing. I was living a lie and wearing a mask and our marriage did not survive the sudden changes that I imposed in our home. We were separated 10 days after the brain hemorrhage and the divorce was finalized in December of that year, 2005. I am happy to declare that it appears she has remarried to a wonderful man and that they are well. Prayers and blessings to them. I did confess from the beginning that I was a mess. Now you are getting a clearer picture of the broken man that showed up in Bruce's office. I was an absolute disaster.

Well, I have been healing emotionally, spiritually, and financially. I've now had almost two years of a great example of what family is all about. It is so embarrassing to admit that I'm approaching 50 years old, and this is something I had never witnessed nor been taught. So grateful to still be alive. Well, that said, one advantage of my broken life is that I now realize that I see things that most people don't. I know, that sounds like a horror movie, right? No, seriously, things that have eternal value are visible to me and more importantly, I can tell that people around me don't see it. Life (not just mine) is about to provide a clear understanding of what eternal looks like. Meeting Bruce, Brenda, and the family was only the beginning.

We are once again sitting in the office and one of our executive co-workers comes to visit and tells this story about a 15-year-old boy who is a friend of her son. Then, after finishing the story, literally asked Bruce to consider adopting this kid. I know, crazy, right? It was with absolute sincerity but met with absolute rejection. I love both, so I won't provide how that played out and potentially insult either of them. That said, Bruce's other kids were adopted with even less notice. Remember, I told you that his family's life story is a movie blockbuster. I am intentionally only hijacking pieces of it. God sent me to an amazing example of how to do it right.

Well, do you see this train wreck developing? After about 30 minutes of sitting in my chair with my back to Bruce's desk and questioning why God had me in this place and why was I privileged to hear that story, I turned my chair and got Bruce's attention and said, "I think I am going to adopt that kid."

You guessed it! Here comes the next lecture. Bruce gets up and closes the door. This door closing expression of privacy is so hypocritical, by now we both know that all it accomplishes is muffling the words. It doesn't provide a hint of concealing that we aren't having a cheerleader competition. Mr. Volume Knob can be heard up and down the halls daily. His volume is just as loud regardless of the topic. It could be football, politics, technology, work, family, and everything else. If the door is open then everyone in the building hears us clearly and without soliciting will receive the option of retelling the story, but if the door is closed then all they know is that Bruce is yelling at Mark again. There were very few days anybody went home without a story to tell. Many times, I would step from my office and co-workers would ask me if I was alright because they had totally misunderstood what all the volume was about. By now, I learned how to handle the volume and not miss his message. The volume is the only way He gives a message. Right or wrong, Bruce has a message and most times, it is eternal.

This sermon was different. It was louder, and it was in defense of the kid. Bruce still had the opinion that I wasn't ready to take on life of this magnitude. This is the big one, this is eternal. This isn't a hobby that you simply lose interest and move on to the next one.

Up to this time in my life, I had not watched much TV. I'm a workaholic and devoted my life to a career and generating revenue. Oh, and because my priorities of life were upside-down, I lost both. Yes, that's the common phrase most people that fail in marriage and business share. Not me. I used to think I lost everything because of not understanding life's (God's) priorities, but I have witnessed many wealthy people still living with their first wife and attend church who haven't a hint of "life's priorities".

I believe my experiences are because He had plans for me from the beginning. My experiences with my Creator are personal. He was never going to allow me to be "that guy". Later, I will share proof that this was His commitment from my beginnings.

Know that the beginning of my life story is an opposing force that questions my decision to begin this book on May 6, 2005, the day of the brain hemorrhage, rather than the big event in July 1965. The brain hemorrhage event was something compatible with being retold at the table. The 1965 event may not ever make it to the printed page.

Bruce continues challenging the physical limits of tenacity as well as my ability to hear. After talking for hours, he realizes, ready or not, that I am going to do this. The conversation changes spirit and now my brother is schooling me. Afterwards, I left and went to pick up the boy. I return and Bruce meets him for the first time, literally 15 minutes after I picked him up. OH MY GOD!

I didn't go to work that day with the intent of adopting a kid. I didn't spend months thinking, praying, or sharing with anyone that I wanted a kid. But I did spend almost two years watching the life of Bruce and Brenda who adopted four kids. I witnessed love and life like I had never seen it before. Neither Bruce nor I knew how well prepared I was for the Master's task, but we did know it was going to be done.

The boy's name is Travis, and he is 15 years old. I picked him up and took him to the office. Craziness, right? Bruce meets Travis for the first time. Travis goes down the hall to the restroom and Bruce's face told me far more than his words. He simply says, "We have a lot of work to do." Did you hear that? He didn't say that I had a lot of work to do, he said WE. Isn't that hilarious. Just a few hours ago he turned down the opportunity and now he has already joined the cause. He is truly a brother. Yes, Brenda is everything we say, but look at this Bruce guy. These two guys are gifts. It's been nearly two years of consistent loving your neighbor as yourself. Travis returns and he and I leave the office.

Oh, you want to know more about Travis? Fasten your seatbelt, this is the scariest roller coaster you will ever ride. Let's just start with the waistline of his pants or should I say the thigh-line. The waistline of his pants was below his crotch and was wearing a fake-diamond blingy belt with the letter F. He had no problem knowing his underwear was revealed. This is my son.

It's Wednesday, February 21, 2007, and Travis is now staying with me at my apartment in Clear Lake. We get up early, jump in Big Red and I drop him off at the high school which is on the way to my work. You think Bruce and I talked that day? Duh! Nobody has my tenacity, so I wouldn't impose to make you read that chapter. I leave work to pick up Travis at school and I am now a bonified good guy, right? Years later the movie Blindside came out. My inspiration was Bruce and Brenda. I am certain there are thousands of stories like mine that don't make it to celebrity status. Someone simply adopts a kid that nobody loves. Blessings to all of you. This is work. This is now my duty. This changed my schedule, my priorities, my career, my finances, and my privacy the following day without notice.

I learned that Travis is a ward of the State of Texas CPS (Child Protective Services), so the next day, the 22nd, he and I visited downtown Houston to get his custody transferred. I learned that the State of Texas provides compensation to offset the cost of guardianship. That helps? I will let you decide. They tell me to return the following day and the guardianship papers will be prepared proving that I am his legal guardian. We leave, I drop him off at school and then go to work. It's another day in paradise and another day with Bruce who is now the most amazing life coach on the planet. I am getting "on the job" training in how to parent an adopted kid from the most qualified teacher on the planet. I believed that then and I still believe that today. My summary of that training is that it is all about how quickly you can connect the dots that play out in your presence. How quickly can you see the story from His eyes? You know your heart is right, but you must see the story to know your participation is required.

On Friday, the 23rd, I drop him off at school and then return to CPS to attain the guardianship papers. I return to Travis's high school with the papers and introduce myself as his new guardian. I was totally not expecting the reaction I received *but life had me 100% prepared. I see the story.*

After presenting my purpose for visiting the school administration department, they immediately retrieved the principal of the school.

"Hello Mr. Stroderd, I am the principal, and we are relieved that somebody is going to assist at getting Travis *through the system.*" Hilarious, right? Ok, so you know me by now. I have been in training for almost two years for a moment like this.

Likely to their satisfaction I replied, "I need his current grades, attendance records, and transfer papers."

There was a pause and a stare. We all realized that we had crossed a line that neither of us could correct. I can only assume that the principal quickly realized she was benefiting by getting rid of the negative statistic and asked, "Which school are you planning for him to transfer."

I replied, "Alvin High School."

She advised, "That requires you to be a resident within that school district."

Quite firmly and confidently I let her know, "I will be by Monday." Yes, I was mad. No, I am not thinking. I haven't a clue how they perceived me.

Looking back and now knowing our statistics driven education system, they might have given each other a high five. Ok, that was rude but here is what they didn't do. They didn't apologize or try to talk me out of it. I was waiting for it and was ready to accept it, but regardless Travis was not spending another day under their authority.

They provided Travis's attendance records, his grades in each class, and the transfer papers needed for me to provide the administrative office in Alvin School District. As they were preparing the packet, I was thinking about how instinctively this took place. I didn't have to take a minute to consider my reaction or my words, it just came out. At that very instant I realized that I was behaving as though he was my DNA son. It was instinctive. I didn't pray for it; I didn't even consider if I would love him more or less than my two daughters, it just happened. He is my son. I took the packet without reading it and headed to my office.

This is the 3rd day that I have had Travis. On the way from high school to the office I had an experience with my Creator that I have never had before and cannot be explained to this day. The moment I walked into the office; Bruce knew about what I was experiencing. My apologies, but the rest cannot be told. You will just have to adopt a kid the way that I did it and then you will likely experience what I experienced. With no measurements, I simply accepted the role of father of a child that nobody wanted. The experience was eternal and priceless. Glory to the King!

I am retelling my story with the principal to Bruce and making myself appear to be a superhero. Then I realized I must move to Alvin this weekend. It is impossible to exaggerate how much Bruce laughed. He would stop laughing to do some work and then bust out laughing again. With the sincerest brother tone he says, "You are so stupid. You have to move to Alvin by Monday."

We continued talking, then I decided to open the packet and learned that Travis's grades were 0, 0 ,7, 12, 19, and 26. His average was about 11-out-of-100. I then reviewed his attendance and learned that he skips almost every class, every day. I learned that he even skipped classes the days that I dropped him off. Poor Travis, this book intentionally conceals almost all the dirty laundry of my life, but not Travis. I'm going to parade his story. His absolutely amazing story!

Yes, after reading the contents of the packet we are loud, but the hypocrisy door is closed. I only wish I could include personal testimony of what it was like to be one of our co-workers. I am betting neither of us fared well with the hall monitors.

Because of Travis's grades we decided to nickname him 007. Ok, so how do I get this boy's attention. He is 15 and must have an immediate change of course in his life. He has got to mature ten years of life within the next three years. I am determined to advance the maturity curve as much as possible TODAY. Surely you understand that after 15 years being dropped off from door to door his entire life that he cannot relate to a father-son conversation yet. I am ready. I have a plan. Let's see how it works.

We are scheduled to visit Travis's previous residency to retrieve the rest of his clothes. It's February so it gets dark around 6pm. Travis goes inside and returns with a huge contractor trash bag. I asked him if those were all his clothes and he replied yes. He is standing at the door of my truck with the door open and I tell him, "Son, I am the last daddy you are ever going to have. Throw your clothes in the back of the truck and get in. There is no quitting! We are going to do this! You understand?"

Poor kid, he is having to make decisions that no kid should ever have to make. He is hearing strangers proclaim to become his dad. How does a kid cope with this? There is so much more that I could share about this moment.

Travis throws the bag in the back of the truck, and we take a ride.

I am now headed to Interstate 45 towards Galveston. My plan requires that the truck speed must be set on cruise at 60 MPH. While on the way, I asked Travis if he had an awesome day at school. He replied, yes. I then apologized for not asking about his classes. I used my newness of becoming a dad as an excuse for forgetting then asked about his math class, "Is your math teacher cool? I love math."

Travis replied, "Yea dad, I love math to. My math teacher is cool."

We continued small talk, and I learned that though he is a boy with few words, he has mastered the skill of telling lies. Finally, I am on I-45 and set the truck on cruise at 60 MPH.

I now reach for my truck side pocket and hand Travis the packet with the proof of the many lies he has just shared. I let him know that he is welcome to open the door and jump out at any time. Now you know why I wanted to be on the interstate and cruising for a long time. Truly, I feared that if the truck stopped before I was finished, he would be tempted to bail. I will spare the details of how that conversation played out and just say that to this day Travis claims his life is scarred from the volume, content, and choice of words that were shared. I call that success!

I challenge you to imagine how our first moments as a father and son played out. It seems that my understanding of his life is having a greater impact on me than my life is impacting him. He gets to eat; I get to grow up.

Christian Hebrew Study – Honor or Kings

It's April 2022 and The Sunday School class is studying God's Moedim. During our last class we revealed that the date Jesus was born was the first Day of Sukkot, one of God's Appointed Times that usually takes place near the end of September on our calendar. More evidence proving this is His birthday will be revealed later but is it required? Once you research the evidence provided earlier, do you require more? Is celebrating His birthday on the correct day of the year important or required? Is it okay to knowingly celebrate it on a different day because it is the intent of the heart that counts more than the legalistic day of the year? Well, almost all of us have received a belated birthday present, even from the ones we love most. Just playback how that felt. Now consider that our Jesus has a reason for everything and imagine what you might have missed at that birthday party. Later we will reveal just how big that party was.

Ok, so Jesus's birthday is in September. Whose birthday is December 25th? Does it really matter? You know, it's a big day for our kids to experience Santa Claus, elfs, Rudolf, Frosty, Grinch, lights, presents, and whatever else fairyland comes up with next. Surely the paganistic nature is quite visible. I believe it to be the most visible of all holidays other than Halloween. So, it doesn't take a crystal ball to see that this isn't good. Those celebrating the birth of baby Jesus on this day are required to share their respects to the Son of God with whomever it is that might have been born on that day. Once again, this holiday became legal in 1870.

Can you imagine the impact on the church when Christmas became a legal holiday. With a little effort you can find evidence of the impact this law had on our country, transforming its loyalty from separation of church and state to the industrial revolution. In 1870 Christmas was not commercialized and its paganistic heritage was well known and not debated. Today, there are almost no religious objections to its celebration. Only the weirdest of the weird openly refuse to participate in the Christmas Season and are faced with a range of judgements from many churches. Some declare them to be deniers of the

Gospel and others view them as legalistic. They teach that honoring Jesus's birthday is a condition of the heart and not the calendar.

Well kids, sadly all of you were grown and out of the house the year your dad learned of the revelation of His birthday in the New Testament. That same year we committed to celebrating His birthday on the correct day. Biblical knowledge has authority over cultural traditions. There is something special about knowing you are celebrating His birthday on His birthday and equally special about **NOT** celebrating His birthday on any other day. His birthday is an Appointed time set on the 4th Day of Creation.

Honor of Kings

The Bible provides us two stories where an Ark is involved. There is the Ark (התבה) that Noah built and there is the Ark (תבת) that Yochobed, Moses's mother, built when Moses was an infant.

Did you know that Yochobed translates to "Glory of God" in English? Can you imagine, "Hello, Ms. Landers, this is my mother, Glory of God. Mom, this is my math teacher, Ms. Landers." Craziness? Again, most (nearly all) proper nouns of scripture were not translated.

The definition of the Hebrew letters of the word Ark that Noah built is, "Behold(ה) the Covenant(ת) of the House(ב) to be Revealed(ה).

Wow! How many ways can you apply that sentence to what you already know about the Story of Noah? What an awesome 15 additional seconds to that video! Add to that, Noah's name means REST. And his name spelled backwards in Hebrew spells the word that means GRACE. Coincidence? No way, right? Now let's look at the Hebrew word Ark in Moses's story.

The Covenant (ת) in the House(ב) of the Covenant(ת)

God promised to send a deliverer to draw them out of Egypt. That promise (covenant) was Moses who was inside the house. Moses's Hebrew name means "To Draw Out".

The Same Story Again These two stories and two words translated as Ark have another unique link not found in many stories of scriptures.

Exodus 2:5 KJV: And the daughter of Pharaoh came down to wash herself at the river; and her maidens walked along by the river's side; and when she saw the ark (התבה) among the flags, she sent her maid to fetch it.

Within the story of the Ark that held Moses, only in Exodus 2:5 does the spelling match the spelling of the word ark in the Noah story. Until learning Hebrew, I had never seen a link between the Ark of these two stories. There are many more, I just decided to share this one because of its uniqueness.

Glory to the King!

Chapter 13

Migdol (מגדל) – Tower

Life

I take the next exit and head back to the apartment. The following morning, we headed to Bruce and Brenda's. We are riding in the red, jacked-up F350 that is now called "Big Red". Oh, and I am wearing a cowboy hat. On the way there I inquired, and Travis confirmed that the bag in the back of the truck contained all his clothes. We stopped at a dumpster at the local Kroger store where I then threw the bag into the dumpster. You should have seen his face. I then told him, "Son, where I come from, we wear our pants above our crotch. Tomorrow, we will get you some new clothes but if I catch you wearing pants below your crotch we will take another drive down the interstate, clear?"

Travis replied, "Yes."

Somehow retelling this story makes me sound way more successful than it really played out. I can only wish every step of these beginnings was as it sounded. That said, they weren't zero percent successful either.

The next morning, I drop Travis off at Bruce and Brenda's house and now I must find a place in Alvin School District to live. I go down main street and cross the railroad tracks and pass the intersection of Hwy 6 for about half a mile. I make a U-turn and then pull over to pray. "God, lead me to the house that I need. In Jesus name, Amen." Yes, I am really good at simple prayers.

I cross Hwy 6, head back into Alvin. I turn right into a neighborhood. It is crucial that you understand that I did not circle back. I literally never made two right turns or left turns. I simply drove without turning back and then I noticed a For Sale by Owner sign. It was amazing. There is a cool-looking little blue house on a corner and across the street from Alvin High School. The address was 715 W Cleveland St.

It was about 10:00am Saturday morning and I dial the number. A sweet-sounding lady answered. I said, "Mam, my name is Mark, and I would like to look at your home for sale."

She replied, "Can we do this Monday?"

I said, "Mam, I have a boy to enroll into the school on Monday and have to move to Alvin this weekend."

She asked, "Are you trustworthy?"

I replied, "Well, I drive a Ford F350 and wear a cowboy hat. Does that count for anything?"

She replied, "The key is under the mat at the back door. Look at the house and let me know."

I walked in and knew immediately that this was the house. I called her back and said, "Mam, is there any way you could meet me today? I want to buy your home and move into it tonight?"

She came and we visited, and I assured her that the loan wasn't going to have any issues. Somehow, she believed me, and we finalized the loan with the title company the following week. Travis and I moved into the house that night.

Is that amazing? I bought a new house before lunch! Was it a good deal? I don't know. It cost a little bit more than Bruce's porch. Thank you, Lord! I'm blown away! Tomorrow Bruce's boys, Link, and Travis are going to help me move from the apartment to the house.

Bruce had taught me a lot about adopted kids. The bottom line is the older they are when you get them, the more work there is to do. Well, Travis is very likely to read this one day, so I will simply declare that he was dealt a tough hand. He was forced to deal with a lifestyle that most can't relate. I am now aware that there are far more people living this way than I had ever imagined. Travis is about 5'8" tall and must weigh at least 130 pounds. Yea, he's a beast!

The house has electricity, it's late February and it's about 40 degrees outside. A breaker trips and I can't seem to get it to reset. It's an old house with old timey fuse boxes that have those screw-in fuses. It's about 9pm and I tell Travis I'm tired and I simply lay on the hardwood floor to go to sleep and Travis does likewise. A few minutes later Travis says, "Hey dad."

I reply, "What up?"

He says, "This floor is hard to sleep on."

I replied, "You know what? It is. Get in the truck."

We jumped in Big Red and headed to the local Walmart that is thankfully open 24 hours a day. We got two blow-up mattresses and one of those blowers to blow them up. I'm headed to checkout and Travis says, "Hey dad, you think we might need a sheet or blanket."

I replied, "You're right." So, we got sheets, blankets, and a pillow.

It's so funny. We get home and Travis realizes that we don't have electricity so we can't blow up the mattresses. I laughed and said, "Dude, you really downsized. You used to have a warm bed to sleep in. Your life sucks!"

We both laughed and I told him to follow me. We take the blower and start plugging into every wall socket until we find one that works. The socket is in the old garage, so we run an extension cord through the house and blow up the mattresses and now WE ARE RICH. We have a place to sleep.

I'm lay there and begin thinking and asked, "Hey Travis."

He replied, "Yea." I'm not kidding, Travis says yes with a tone and enunciation like I have never heard before.

I said, "You know, if you are my son, I guess I should know your name. What's your whole name?"

He replies, "Travis Garrett Demas."

I replied, "No way, your last name is dumbass?"

He replied, "No! Demas." We laugh and I go back to trying to sleep.

About five minutes later Travis says, "Hey dad."

I replied, "Yes."

He tells me, "I'm hungry."

I replied, "Me to. Let's go."

It was about midnight and once again, we jumped in Big Red. Thankfully our local Kroger is also open 24x7. We walk the aisles and Travis gets a bag of those white powder donuts and some milk. I totally forgot what I got. We get home and he is laying on his newly customized blow-up mattress and eating those donuts. I look over and all I can see is his big lips covered in white powder.

It's Sunday and we got everything moved. Now Travis and I are at the local Cowboy store getting him some clothes for school. All I can do is laugh as I tell the story. This kid was wearing gangsta clothes and now he is standing in a cowboy store. Yes, we get him what he needs but just seeing his 0% cowboy spirit talking to the sales lady that is 100% cowgirl is the video of the day.

It's Monday and Travis and I make an early visit to Alvin School District administration office. Done! Travis is enrolled! Amazing! I drop him off at school and go to work. Perfect!

I get home around the time that school lets out and then Travis gets home. He has a friend. You know, I never included friends in my preparations. Travis introduces us, "Hey dad, this is Dederick. Dederick this is my dad, Mark."

We shared some small talk and Dederick is quick to being comfortable and just being himself. The guy is beyond cool. A few minutes later Dederick asked, "Mr. Mark, you want to see my underwear? I stole them from ABC place."

I turned around and got a nonconfrontational grip on his shirt and asked him to follow me. I took him to the door, opened it, and assisted him to stand outside my door, then replied, "Son, do you know why people steal?"

He replied, "No sir."

I answered, "Because they don't trust God to provide their needs. Get out of my house."

I went back to the kitchen and finished cooking hamburger helper for me and Travis. Yes, you are about to learn about my amazing cooking skills. Remember? It's all about the food.

You are not going to believe this. The next day Travis comes home and Dederick is with him. Dederick walks in and immediately starts talking, "Mr. Mark, look here. My grandpa is a bishop. If he found out that I stole something he would remove a layer of hide off my butt. My family doesn't steal. I don't know what made me do it, but I promise I will never do it again."

I replied, "Cool, get you a plate and let's eat."

A few minutes later Bruce pulls up and his two boys James and Jacob are with him. They come in and grab a plate and we are all sitting in the living room talking and eating. Sure enough, a few minutes later, Link walks in and gets a plate and starts eating. Yep, you guessed it. About an hour later, here comes Brenda. She walks in and gets a plate and here we go! We are doing what we do best, eating and talking. Life is good!

The next day Bruce and I got home, and I told everyone let's go to Kroger. We have to fill this house with food. So, Jacob, James, and Travis walk into Kroger, and I tell them to go get whatever they want. Uncle Mark is buying. Well, Travis is still trying to figure out this new life he has committed to. Jacob and James each take a basket and they are excited. Travis grabs a basket and walks slowly behind me and Bruce. He hasn't put anything in his basket yet until we get to this display rack of Little Debbie cakes. It is impossible to write or tell this slow enough to mimic the slothful speed of Travis's movements. Stop! You are reading too fast. He is moving crazy slow. Bruce and I are just watching to see how this clown show plays out.

Travis grabs a box of Little Debbie cakes and puts it in the basket. I estimate that took at least 20 seconds. Then he looks at us while we say nothing, and he does it again. Yes, another 20 seconds. I feel like I am witnessing grocery store yoga. He looks at us again and gets no sign of rejection or implying he can't have more. He then stands in front of the display and wraps his arms around the entire shelf to grab as many as possible at one time and then slowly drops them carefully into the basket. I'm guessing there were at least 20 boxes. He looks at us with a grin as though he just accomplished some record-breaking athletic achievement. Bruce and I look at each other and Bruce with the most nonchalant voice says, "That boy likes Little Debbie cakes."

We get home and Brenda is there. She sees that I am not done unpacking, so we are unpacking and it's February, daylight savings time so it gets dark around 6pm. We are talking and unpacking. Bruce is still stunned that I got a new home across from the high school in four hours. While we are just unpacking and talking, we know that the morons (James, Jacob, Travis, Link, Dederick (the bishop), and a few others) are outside acting like a pack of fools, but that's what 9th graders do, right?

Next thing you know; they walk into the house and Travis's face is all bloody. Bruce and I are trying to get the boys to talk one at a time. Some are talking while the others are laughing. Voices and laughter are echoing.

Ok, so it sounds like they were playing some game and Travis was running and literally ran full speed, face-first into a chain-link fence. Well, while Bruce and I were getting the story, Brenda is in the kitchen assessing the damage. Did I mention she was a nurse! You should have seen it. Within a minute, amidst the loud chaos, she has Travis in a chair in the middle of the kitchen. His face is cleaned off and she has her list of what I need to pick up at the pharmacy.

I got back and within minutes the entire scenario was reduced to competition between the boys of the best retelling of the story at school the next day. If I remember the winning story was that Travis was jumped by a group of gangsters and if you think he looks bad, you should see what he did to those guys. After the healing was done, he ended up with one little beauty mark on his smooth face. Oh, I forgot to share, Travis is a "pretty boy". I had no idea. In just three days in Alvin, his personality is coming out. Mr. 007 is a hilarious mess. Remember, we named him 007 because his grades were 0, 0, 7, 12. 19, 26.

Normal life is I go to work while Travis gets ready and goes to school (literally across the street). The gang meets at the house after school, then me and Bruce show up, we wait on Brenda, and then everybody goes to eat. The boys have gotten the sermon that 715 is a dude ranch. Remember, the house address is 715 W Cleveland St. We just called it 715. The boys include Jacob, James, Link, Travis, Dederick (the bishop), and occasionally a couple of spares. We were feeding anybody that got in the trucks. We would load up two F350's and go eat.

I only had Travis about two weeks and it's time to go to the airport to pick up my daughter who I fly in to visit twice a month. By this time Travis and I are buds. It takes a couple years for all the "father-son" stuff to be natural and permanent. Well, that's if the family is normal. This family isn't normal and the craziest of the bunch is about to get in the truck. My crazy daughter Anna is one year younger than Travis and is a walking light bulb. Like one of those floodlights at road construction sites. She is a mess! By the way, I did not give Travis any warnings about Anna. That might have been a mistake.

It's late and dark outside. Anna sees Big Red and throws her stuff in the bed. Travis has been kind enough to have already moved to the back seat to let his new sister sit with her dad. Let me try to remember how long it took for Anna to take us to a place we thought we would never go. Oh yea, two seconds. She gets in the truck, closes her door, looks in the back seat at Travis and says, "So, you are my new brother?"

Travis replies with that mixed Alvin influenced ghetto and says, "Yea."

Anna replies, "Wow, you got really big lips."

Okay, here we go! It's only uphill from here, right? Well, like I said, only Anna could say that. Everybody is laughing so hard they can't talk. I can't remember where the conversation went from there but the "Let me get to know you part" took five seconds. These two visited like brother and sister from the first second. I would quickly learn that the two of them have similar personalities. Both are goofballs.

A few nights a week, Uncle Mark would cook his custom hamburger helper recipe. Not kidding, we must feed between 5-10 teenage football players so I would use this huge gumbo pot. It was a custom mixture because I had to add more meat to feed more kids which then required more hamburger helper. Man, my Louisiana heritage was paying off. I would grab my extra packages of cheese then estimate the pounds of extra ground meat so I would…**ok, you get it?** I started with hamburger helper but had no clue what it would be when I was done. James always loved it. The joke is that James, the moose, would eat anything.

There was one night where the portions of ingredients rebelled against me, and it looked like the cheese was behaving like Elmers's glue and keeping everything stuck together like a popcorn ball. It was hilarious to watch each kid pass by the pot and emphatically declare "I ain't eating that!". Well, all but James. He stuck the metal serving spoon to scoop some in his plate and it looked like the entire pot stuck to the spoon like a basketball. That didn't bother James. He was able to carve out what he wanted and sat down and had himself a wonderful meal. It's impossible to imitate the conversation of five teenage morons. It was another day in paradise. All I remember is Bruce saying, "I ain't eating that. Get in the truck, let's go to Tapa."

There was someone spending the night almost every night. Mr. 007 actually attended school without skipping and did his homework. The place became the hangout. We never knew how many kids were going to be at the house when we got home. All we required is no drugs, no damaging the property, no girls, no fights, and no hospitals.

You aren't going to believe this. Bruce and I got home at 715 and found out it was report-card day. Mr. 007 has all A's and B's, except for two 50's. Mr. 007 has a new name. Now we call him 50/50. You guessed it! Let's Go To Tapa! Let's eat! My son is passing five out or seven classes. Craziness! Impossible to exaggerate how much fun we are having. The local restaurants love us, Bruce and I are generous tippers and appreciate them tolerating our morons.

Christian Hebrew study

I enjoy transitioning between the different times of my life while telling these stories. I mentioned earlier that we live in a little cabin on the side of a hill in Medina, Tx but what I didn't share is that this little cabin used to be a chicken coop. I am not kidding. The little chicken door that looks like a doggy door is still on the front screen door. Prior to being a chicken coop, it was a hunting cabin. The cabin does not have any closets and the kitchen has three counter tops that are each about one foot wide. I'm not kidding. Wait, it gets better. It has a room and a full bath upstairs, but the stairs are not safe, and the ceiling follows the roofline of the house, so you must tilt your head to one side to get to the second floor. Stop laughing! Since we chose to use the upstairs for storage, and the small room downstairs for our closet and pantry, that left only one room downstairs for our bedroom, living room, dining room, and laundry. Yes, all of that is in a 12'x24' room. We left a 3,600 Sq Ft barndominium that was amidst an additional 1,800 Sq Ft expansion when we sold to move here. We are crazy content, and you should see the faces of visitors, especially our kids, when they visit. It is slightly bigger than a modern "Tiny-House" and we absolutely love it.

Well, it's the beginning of May 2022 and Sunday School is finishing the Moedim series. I am proud of my boldness to tell the truth but waiting to have my wings clipped. I am truly stunned by the acceptance of my research and teaching. We are still maintaining 30-40 attendees. Most importantly my sweet Lisa is always with me. Now that you know about the cabin then you understand just how sweet she is.

The easy way to understand God's Appointed Times, His Moedim, is to compare it to our modern-day holidays. The only difference is that our National Holidays, even the few that fall on the same day of the year as His Moedim, have a totally different purpose. Each chapter is laying foundation to build upon. As we continue this book series, God's Moedim will become more beautiful and many that read this book will wonder why they had never heard of God's Moedim or God's Appointed Times.

Honor of Kings

The story of having to move to Alvin reminds me of the names of towns in scripture which are also not translated into English. There is a town named Migdol (מגדל) which is where Moses stood when God (יהוה) parted the waters and the mixed multitude (all nations) crossed over on dry land. We are very familiar with the Crossing of the Red Sea story, but few are familiar with the name of the town where Moses stood and even fewer are familiar with its significance.

There is another very familiar New Testament story about a lady named Mary who was the first to witness that Jesus was not in the tomb. Until learning Hebrew and the significance of the town named Migdol (מגדל), I never considered the extent of the privilege of being the first to witness our Savior's Resurrection granted to Mary. Because there are so many women in the New Testament named Mary, rarely is this Mary's name mentioned without including the town she is from. She is commonly referenced as Mary Magdalene. For many decades I considered Magdalene to be her last name. Somewhere in my past I learned that Mary Magdalene is Mary from Magdala. People from Magdala are called Magdalene's. From my Hebrew studies I then learned that Magdala is the Aramaic name of the town and the Hebrew word for Magdala is Migdol (מגדל).

Now I have two of the most well-known people of scripture that are both associated with a town by the same name. One is in the Old Testament, and one is in the New Testament. By now we know that the link is concealed within the revelations of the Hebrew letters that spell Migdol. But before revealing that understanding let's consider something I believe to be special when comparing these two people.

Moses's name in Hebrew is Moshe (משה) which means To Draw Out. His name spelled backwards is Hashem (השמ) which means "The (ה) Name (שמ)". Just when you thought that Moses couldn't be more special. Mary Magdalene on the other hand is described as a woman with seven devils. Because seven is the number that represents perfection, I view her description as being the perfect sinner. Mary had the perfect number of devils. Could you possibly choose two people further apart on the spectrum of holiness?

God (יהוה) chose Moses (משה) to lead the people out of Egypt which is commonly referred to as "The World". And He chose the perfect sinner to be the first to observe that His son had left this world.

The definition of the Hebrew letters that spell Migdol (מגדל) is,

Those Born of Flesh (Womb) (מ) Receive Wealth (ג) From the Door (ד) of Him who has Authority(ל)

The Same Story Again The Moses, Mary, and Migdol story could make a great sermon. I wish I would have understood Migdol in my formative years as a Christian. The story would have provided more proof that Jesus is the same yesterday, today, and forever. I would be first in line to buy a ticket to see this story added to one of those late 1950's movies telling the stories of Moses and Jesus.

The Same Story Again This story has more revelations when you research the two Hebrew words spelled by the first two letters and the last two letters. The first two letters spell Mig (מג) which is in scripture twice and seems to be related to great wealth and the last two letters spell Dol (דל) which is in the scripture twenty-one times and is translated as poor. An alternative definition of the Hebrew letters is, "For those born (מ) of the flesh to become rich (ג), they must walk through a door (ד) that leads to becoming poor in spirit, giving authority (ל) of life to the Savior (ישוע)."

The Same Story Again My understanding of Numbers 33:1-7 is that Moses encamped at Migdol in Egypt on the 3rd Day after leaving Rameses. Mary from Migdol in the promised land visited the tomb on the 3rd Day. These two events took place on the exact same date on the calendar. Coincidence?

Chapter 14

Sukkot (סכת) – Booth or Tabernacle

Life

Well, it's time to get some muscle on this skinny kid. We went to Academy, and I told him to get a shopping basket and fill it with whatever he wants. He got a basket and walked away while I enjoyed shopping. About five minutes later he meets me and all he has in his basket is a football. Can you believe that? He was given a blank check at Academy and came back with a football.

I am really surprised. What do I do? I tell him, "Follow me."

I decided that we would walk each aisle together and see if the football is really all he wants. The first aisle was weights. We went to the dumb bells, and I said, "Dude, pick up that 25-pound weight." He picks it up and then I said, "Curl it."

He replies, "I can't."

I replied, "Yes, I know, put it in the basket."

I took him around the store, and we got tennis shoes, cleats, clothes, socks, a basketball, and anything else that I could convince him to want. Yes, the key is that I was convincing him to want stuff that he never considered having or using.

I have been told many times that I make strange faces when I am thinking. Whether I am programming, reading, listening, or even meditating I am unaware that I make faces. No, I don't mean something silly or stupid. I am just one of those people that cannot hide when the wires in my head are firing. I have been interrupted many times by people watching me work. Well, while driving home from Academy, I am sure that Travis witnessed me making faces. He has no idea how showing up with nothing but a football in his basket impacted me. Just make your own "thinking" face and figure it out. What's in this kid's head? How is he wired?

We get home and the clan shows up. Travis and Dederick are talking about how black people have darker or lighter skin color. I expressed that I had been around black people my entire life and had never heard of such a thing. The conversation continues and gets crazy humorous. When it's all done, Dederick (the bishop) has the nickname, Hazelnut. These kids are nuts!

Absolutely crazy nuts! But they are good kids, and nobody is breaking the Dude Ranch rules. 715 is a safe house.

Over the next few months, we have established an unscheduled weekly pattern. Anyone would love to spend a day with us but almost nobody could maintain the pace. Life is *Ramped Up*! Never a dull moment.

It's April 2007 and I decided to join a dating service. Joining was an absolute pain. I can't remember how many questions I had to answer but I think it was over four hundred. While answering the questions I realized that every lady on this site had to answer these questions also. After realizing that, I was excited about the questions. It made sense. They ask me all the questions that everybody wants answered but doesn't know how to ask.

I'm all done and published my profile. The next night the dating site had a lady trying to contact me. So, I communicated with this lady via their software, and she replied. After a few communications we exchanged phone numbers and then after talking a few times we decided it's time to visit.

It's May 6, 2007, exactly two years since the brain hemorrhage, and I asked Bruce and Brenda to watch Travis so that I could go on a date.

I leave the house on my green KLR650 with my orange flag flying to meet this lady at her son's baseball game at Pearland High School. She didn't know where the school was located so I had her meet me at a crossroad and I would escort them to the game. We met and she followed but when I pulled into the school parking lot there was this huge snapper turtle in the driveway. I get off my bike and do my Louisiana Tarzan imitation and carry the turtle to the nearby ditch.

Did you know that there is a Tarzan exhibit at a museum in Morgan City, Louisiana? Yes, the Louisiana Atchafalaya Basin is where the first Tarzan movies were filmed. Ok, I digress.

We park and go sit down to watch the game. It only took two minutes to realize how shy, meek, sweet, and quiet she was. She is exactly like I perceived her to be over the phone. Her name is Lisa, and she is totally unaware of how beautiful she is. I talked a lot, she talked very little and then it happened, I asked her a question about herself. I watched as this angelic person struggled trying to say a single word about herself. As I watched, I totally fell in love with this lady. We left the game, and I returned home to get Travis.

I walked into the house and Brenda, the greatest sister on the planet, asked, "How'd it go?"

I replied, "I'm going to marry that lady."

Bruce, knowing my marriage failure rate, replies, "You're an idiot."

We all laughed and then I let them know that she is coming tomorrow (Wednesday) to watch the movie Facing the Giants with me. You guys can meet her.

As fate would have it, that afternoon we had our first violation of the Dude Ranch rules. Bruce is doing that Bruce thing where you make the pain so great that nobody will challenge the rule again and right in the middle of his valiant effort this little white Honda Civic parks along the road and beautiful Lisa steps out of the car and walks to the front door. At the same moment, Bruce is apologizing (not required) for the disruption and walking out the backdoor. I went to the door and let Lisa into the house. She was carrying a small vase of begonias and a tub of homemade chocolate chip cookies for Travis.

I said, "Come in. Hey Travis, come meet Lisa. She brought you some cookies. Lisa, this is my friend Bruce's wife, Brenda. I'll take the begonias and put them over here."

Lisa replied, "They are gardenias."

I took the flowers while Lisa and Brenda greeted each other. Then Lisa immediately became the Lisa I met. I am watching two angels meet for the first time. I'm not kidding. This isn't me making some lovey-dovey choice of words. These two ladies are different. Crazy different.

As I watched Lisa and Brenda visit, it felt like I was the visitor. Lisa is talking to Brenda with complete ease. They find out that each of them has two Dachshunds. So, I am watching and notice that they both have blondish hair, and they are both beautiful ladies. I'm thinking to myself, "Wow Brenda, this is a record. Within 15 seconds a total stranger is now your sister." A few minutes later Brenda said her goodbyes so that Lisa and I could watch the movie and visit.

After the visit, Lisa said she would come back tomorrow night and cook Travis and I dinner. Yay!

Of course, Bruce and I talked about Lisa at work. Bruce got the scoop from Brenda and was looking forward to tonight's dinner visit.

It was awesome, Lisa arrived before everyone and is still cooking when everyone shows up. I failed to let the family know that she was just cooking for me and Travis. Anyways, she has this plate of salmon over to the side while she is visiting with Brenda. The family is showing up one at a time. Big James walks into the kitchen and sees these little salmon patties. Bruce and I know what he is thinking as he walks over and is overheard asking, "Is that for all of us?"

This is a HUGE moment. First, it was funny beyond explanation. Lisa is about to find out that we always eat together and that would require a lot more than she had prepared. I should have let her know that, but I didn't. Now we are facing this moment where either Bruce's family is not eating with us, or we are going to put the salmon in the refrigerator and go eat. The bottom line is that we are facing an immediate change of plans.

So, the scenario somehow becomes obvious, and Brenda begins apologizing while Lisa is explaining this was our dinner. It is impossible to explain how Lisa and Brenda are talking but there is zero malice and there is zero judgment. They are truly just telling the truth about what just happened, and nobody is upset. It's so weird. It's only weird because nobody was mad. If this would have happened in my past there would have been yelling and screaming and blaming and…and…and.

While James, the absolute gentleman, is standing next to us and apologizing for saying that to loud, me and Bruce are laughing and letting him off the hook. We have a room full of amazing people experiencing a simple interruption and it is being handled like A SIMPLE INTERRUPTION. Nobody is mad. Everybody has a smile on their face during these conversations. Nobody is making it bigger than it deserves. That is amazing!

Then it happened! Bruce stops laughing and shouts the family motto, "Get in the truck and let's go to Tapa (the local Mexican Food Restaurant)." It's all about the food!

We all get to Tapa and now my sweet Lisa is experiencing our family routine for the first time. But, good news, she is sitting across from Brenda. It is impossible to lose if Brenda is at the table. It's cheating. You would marry me just to have access to Brenda. Everybody tolerates me, Bruce, and the morons because Brenda is with us. We had a crazy good time as Lisa got to know the family. Now she knows that every meal includes the extended family. It was another fun family dinner.

I got to the office the next day and Bruce is shocked that a lady that beautiful and that sweet is available for an idiot like me. We are laughing about Lisa's first experience in the 715 kitchen. Lisa got to meet James, the moose, and his appetite. It was a good day.

Christian Hebrew Study

It's May 2022 and my teaching schedule for Sunday School was shared with one of the Elders that taught spiritual gifts for three weeks. It was an awesome teaching and I returned to teaching Sunday School on the last week of the month.

That class on the last weekend of May was so much fun. We shared our story in the Bible where the role of the donkey is concealed. Yes, in addition to the concealed purpose of the donkey in the triumphal entry told in Chapter 4, let's search out another awesome story about our Savior that is concealed within His purpose of a donkey.

The purpose of this story is to search out a character trait of our Savior that His enemy can't mimic. Surprise, His enemy can mimic Him in many ways. To accomplish this understanding we are going to search out two references to breastplates in the Bible. I am aware that these stories are not as common as others we have discussed so I will provide a little extra detail.

The most common breastplate that we will search out is the one worn by the High Priest. The details of how the breastplate is constructed are in Exodus Chapter 28. The key point for our story is to know that there are twelve precious stones mounted on the breastplate. They are set with four rows and each row has three stones and each stone has engraved a name of one of the twelve sons of Jacob, also known as the 12 tribes of Israel.

The second breastplate is not common knowledge in the Bible. It is in Ezekiel Chapter 38, and it is worn by the King of Tyre. Let's read Ezekiel 28:13.

Ezekiel 28:13 KJV: Thou hast been in Eden the garden of God; every precious stone was thy covering, the sardius, topaz, and the diamond, the beryl, the onyx, and the jasper, the sapphire, the emerald, and the carbuncle, and gold: the workmanship of thy tabrets and of thy pipes was prepared in thee in the day that thou wast created.

Yes, you read that correctly. It appears that the King of Tyre is another name for the devil. And he wore a breastplate that had nine stones! Craziness, right? If you go through the exercise of identifying which stones are on both breastplates you will conclude that the three stones that are not on the King of Tyre's breastplate are the stones that represent the tribes of Gad, Asher, and Issachar. Let's search out the blessings of these three tribes and determine if they represent the character of our Savior that His enemy is unable to mimic. Beautiful thought, right?

- Gad – "*Genesis 49:19…but he shall overcome at the last.*" Jesus will conquer the enemy in the end. The enemy does not possess power over us.
- Asher – "*Genesis 49:20 … his bread shall be fat, and he shall yield royal dainties.*" Fruitfulness, the enemy will never be fruitful. Asher yields royal seed (dainties) and the enemy will never be crowned with royalty.

Genesis 49:14-15 KJV: [14]Issachar is a strong donkey couching down between two burdens: [15]And he saw that rest was good, and the land that it was pleasant; and bowed his shoulder to bear, and became a servant unto tribute.

There is the donkey! Considering that Jacob's son's names are written on the gates of New Jerusalem, then is it possible that Jacob's blessings of his twelve sons is related to the character of our Savior? If so, then the blessing of Issachar reveals that our Savior is willing to bear your burden and His enemy will never bear your burden.

Verse 15 tells us that "…rest was good, and the land was pleasant;…". Could that possibly be referencing the Millennial Rest where the curse from the fall of man is done away? Could the two burdens in Verse 14 be the end of one age (6000 years) and the beginning of a new age (the Millennium)?

Honor of Kings

The Hebrew word for Tabernacle is Sukkot (סכת). Sukkot is another of the Hebrew words that authors have written volumes of books. I will reduce those books to a few pages, which means I will not do this word justice. I can only hope to get you on the path and introduce the depth of the journey.

Sukkot is one of God's Appointed times. We shared earlier that the Feast of Sukkot is also known as The Feast of Tabernacles and The Feast of Booths. Sukkot is the only feast that lasts eight days. It begins on Jesus's birthday and ends on His circumcision which is also referred to as the Great 8th Day or the beginning of eternity. I can still remember how strange the phrase "beginning of eternity" was to me the first time I heard it. Let's review a few instances of Sukkot referenced in scripture.

I believe it is common knowledge that Egypt represents the world and that the Exodus from Egypt is synonymous with leaving this world. The Exodus story includes Passover, the day the death angel passed over the houses that had blood over their doorpost. The Moedim of Passover is six months from the Moedim of Sukkot, but we see in Exodus 12:37 that the first place they camp after leaving Egypt is a town called Sukkot (KJV spells it Succoth). Ok, we will make sense out of this, but I want to create confusion to prove a point.

Exodus Chapter 12 and 13 provide us a lot of detail of the events that took place after the passing of the first born of Egypt. They leave Egypt and camp at a place with the same name as one of God's Appointed Times that takes place six months later. Surely you agree that this is odd. Also, this is on the 3rd day after Passover. Research that and make sure you agree. The death angel passes and the next day they allow Egypt to mourn its dead. The 2nd day they gather their belongings and collect the wealth of Egypt. On the 3rd day they depart and camp at Sukkot. Since this is three days after Passover, then this camp should have been named something resembling three days after the crucifixion. The town should have a name that resembles the word "Resurrection" or "First Fruits". Okay, now let's look at Exodus 13:20-21.

Exodus 13:20-21 KJV: 20And they took their journey from Succoth, and encamped in Etham, in the edge of the wilderness.

21And the LORD went before them by day in a pillar of a cloud, to lead them the way; and by night in a pillar of fire, to give them light; to go by day and night:

Verse 21 shows us that the Lord led the way. Anytime the Lord dwells with us it is consistently referred to as Sukkot which means He tabernacles with us. Even though it was three days after Passover, it was named Sukkot because the Lord tabernacled with them. A sukkot is a temporary dwelling.

It's no surprise that Mary and Joseph were unable to dwell in standard accommodations during the birth of Jesus. Jesus was born in a temporary dwelling, a sukkot. They had to find a covering (booth) where Mary could deliver the baby. Jesus was born in a temporary dwelling (Sukkot) on the first Day of Sukkot, and we are led to understand that He will return on this day as well, The Feast of Sukkot (Tabernacles, Booths).

Glory to the King!

Chapter 15

Et (את) – The First and the Last

Life

I can only estimate that it's June 2007 and living at 715 W Cleveland is on the way to work from Bruce's house. From the time Travis and I moved there Bruce, and I often rode our bikes to work together.

One day at work it was required that I write a small program using C-Programming language which I didn't know. Bruce and I talk about it, and he simply tells me that it looks like I need to learn how to write code in that programming language. The debate begins on whether I will learn how to write in that language or whether we will contract someone that already knows. That debate continues for days, and that broken volume knob somehow gets louder each day, and now we are no longer debating but rather we are truly yelling insults at each other. What's most uncommon about this debate is that Bruce is arguing that I am far more intelligent than I am aware, and he is only irritated that my past has influenced my life negatively. He is irritated because I won't try. Isn't that hilarious. So, my argument is that people go to school for years to learn how to do this.

Okay, so now we are both as mad as we can get. While riding our bikes to work, every time we stop at a red light we aren't behaving like brothers. Finally with pure madness and without an ounce of kindness, I told him that I would do it.

Now I am working with anger each day and we aren't talking. With the most anger that you can imagine, after four days I had learned what I needed to know and had finished the program and it worked perfectly. I must admit that I had no idea that I had that ability.

Then Bruce tells me, *"Whoever is the best brain surgeon in the world better be damn glad that you didn't want to be a brain surgeon. Don't you ever question the gift that God gave you again. I've never met anyone like you."*

We both wear cowboy hats, and we are now sitting in our office with happy tears. We are laughing and he closes the door out of fear that a co-worker would see us crying with our hats on. We are laughing and sharing more beautiful life stories. I am sharing words from my heart that had been bottled up my entire life. I relive that moment often. I have shared that "brain surgeon" quote more times than I can count, even with my own children which makes it crazy special.

What's next? When is this class finished?

Thanks again, Brucie.
I love you, man!

Christian Hebrew Study

It's time to go back to the first day I began studying Hebrew. I hope this helps and motivates everyone to do this. My understanding is that more than four million Christians in the USA know how to read and/or study Hebrew. I am far from unique.

It's September 20, 2021, the first day after attending that first Saturday Bible study and now I begin my efforts to learn Hebrew. I was advised to learn the Hebrew letters and that by simply learning the letters I would be able to start reading and understanding. They also advised me of the best YouTube channels that teach the letters. If you don't know me by now, know that during the next 45 days I watched all the videos from all the channels they referenced. That said, I noticed while watching that there was often another channel referenced on YouTube and it was named Dutch Uncle John. This is the guy!

The first letter of the Hebrew alphabet is the letter Alef (א). After watching the teaching on the letter א (Alef) on all other channels, I decided to watch the teaching on Dutch Uncle John. The teacher's name is John Kostik. I found his teaching style to be so incredibly unique. I experienced what became a common emotional roller coaster during that 71-minute video on the letter Alef (א). Lisa watched as what I was learning made me laugh, cry, happy, and sometimes mad. I was literally shocked at what I learned about the use of a single Hebrew letter. I would only get mad when I considered how old I am before learning this.

I am certain that none of my past Christian brothers would take credit for influencing my prior views of what studying Hebrew meant. That said, almost none have encouraged me to continue my study. Almost none will tolerate hearing what I have learned. Almost all have expressed their concern that I will walk away from my salvation in the Gospels of my Savior. Many have even accused me of being a Judaizer and not believing in Jesus. Wow! So far, all I have done is learn the alphabet of my Father's language.

Can you imagine what it was like being my wife? Poor Lisa. Everyone that knows Lisa, knows that they have met one of the most angelic people that God (יהוה) ever breathed life into. We were married 14 years when I began attending this Christian Hebrew Bible study and then immediately started studying Hebrew. On this first occasion of watching me cry and others to follow, Lisa would simply ask me what I learned that made me cry or made me mad. It took me months to realize that only people that truly love you will ask about Christian Hebrew Bible study with the intent to truly listen. Both of us finally concluded that my abbreviated explanation of the video could not properly represent the content and method of teaching. My loving wife willfully decided to invest her time and energy to follow me down this path of learning Hebrew. Wow, what a wife!

John's videos include teachings of words and Bible stories that the letter being taught is used. I don't know why he does it, but I do know what that did to me. Learning Hebrew doesn't change salvation; it simply provides more clarity of the character of my Savior and Creator. It truly provides insight of the character, to say otherwise would be a lie. It eliminates the issue of trying to learn from over one hundred different English translations that many times don't agree. That said, I will commit to not communicating my personal convictions from these teachings but will commit to explaining what I learned and how it impacted my daily life.

One of the first things I learned was that each Hebrew letter is somehow related to the letters adjacent to the letter. So, the first letter of Hebrew is Alef (א) and it is related to the second letter which is the Bet (ב), and the Alef (א) is also related to the last letter of Hebrew which is the Tav (ת). As mentioned many times already, Alef (א) is the God letter and the Tav (ת) is the Covenant letter. The old Paleo Hebrew pictograph of the Covenant letter is the Cross. It resembles one person making their mark and then the other person making theirs and the result is a cross. Coincidence?

The Same Story Again The Hebrew word Et (את) is spelled from Right-to-Left Alef-Tav, the first letter and the last letter of the Hebrew alphabet.

Revelation 22:13 KJV: I am Alpha and Omega, the beginning and the end, the first and the last.

In Revelation 22:13 Jesus, whose Hebrew name is Yeshua (ישוע), declares Himself to be the first and the last using the Greek alphabet. The

Hebrew equivalent to Alpha and Omega is the Alef (א) and the Tav (ת) which is the word Et (את). What is MOST INTERESTING about this word את is that it is in the Hebrew Old Testament (Tanakh) more than 7,000 times and it is within the Greek New Testament using the first and last letters of the Greek Alphabet, Alpha and Omega (ΑΩ), more than 4,000 times, yet nearly all the occurrences of this word are not translated in the English translations. I have only found that the Expanded Bible (EXB) provides any acknowledgement that the word exists by displaying a very faint dot where it occurs.

The Same Story Again Behold, this knowledge does not change what we already know, but it does enhance the plot. Let's review how our Creator used the Alef-Tav - Et (את) to add additional impact to the plot of other stories that many of us are familiar.

In the original Hebrew text, Ruth's name is simply the word Ruth (רות) until she is redeemed by Boaz and at that time her name is Alef Tav-Ruth (את-רות). It is as though our Savior is placing a stamp on His Word throughout the scriptures.

Again, in the original Hebrew text both Jacob and his brother Esau have Et (את) before their names until after Esau sells his birthright to Jacob. From that moment the Et (את) is no longer before Esau's name.

In the original Hebrew text Jonah's name does not have the Et (את) before his names until Jonah 1:15 where he is "lifted up" to be tossed into the sea. From the time Jonah is lifted-up to the time that the fish vomits him upon the shore, his name is Alef Tav Jonah (את-יונה).

The stories of Alef-Tav are endless and not surprising that the occurrence of Alef-Tav begins in Genesis 1:1 where the word Et (את) stands alone twice in the verse but with a bit of uniqueness. I can only estimate that I have spent more than one hundred hours studying the original Hebrew of Genesis 1:1. There is literally that much to unpack and all of it is beautiful.

Genesis 1:1

בְּרֵאשִׁית בְּרָא אלהים אֶת השמים וְאֶת הָאָרֶץ

HAARETZ V'ET HASHAMAYIM ET ELOHIM BARA BERESHET

Hebrew is read right to left so notice that Et (את) is in the verse twice. Notice also that the 2nd time it has the letter Vav (ו) in front. The Vav (ו) represents the Straight Up Man with the Nail. Would you find it interesting to learn that the word Hashamayim (השמים) means "the heavens" and the word HaAretz (הארץ) means "earth" and the word Et (את), the "First and the Last", is before each of them? Does that change your salvation? Well of course not! Does it make you adore the genius of your Creator's language? Yes! Does it bring adoration to the words of John, "In the beginning was the word…" Of course it does. My increased revelation brings added adoration for *The Word* and brings new understanding to *The Word* becoming *Flesh*. The refreshing complexity of *The Word* is beginning to resemble my idea of the complexity of the DNA.

ET – The First and the Last - את
The First(א) and the Last(ת), God's Covenant(את).

My Savior is referenced with את more than 11,000 times in the original scriptures, and I was not aware of it until learning Hebrew. There is an alternative teaching that denies the divine purpose of את. Is it possible that these are the same people that influenced the word את not to be revealed in the English translations?

Why did You show this to me? Thank you, bless my efforts to share.

Glory to the King!

Chapter 16

Yonah (יונה) – Jonah "Dove"

Life

It's still May 2007, only a couple weeks after everyone met Lisa. She is adapting well. Lisa has two boys, the oldest is Carter who is a junior in high school and Kyle who is a freshman like Travis and both of Bruce's boys. Bonds happen fast when you are old.

I remember calling Lisa at her home in Richmond, Tx and she was crying. While talking to her I learned that her dryer had broken and what was not said but obvious is that she was experiencing a financial struggle. So, without notifying her, I jump in Big Red and head to her house. We are still getting to know each other but it was only slightly weird that I showed up without notice.

I knocked on the door and when she answered I said, "Hi, get what you need and come take a ride with me."

She gets in the truck and asks, "Where are we going?"

I replied, "To get you a dryer."

I could tell this was a good thing. To this day I jokingly get jealous when she sees another man driving a truck with appliances in the back.

Lisa gets it. She quickly grew roots in the family. She is Brenda Junior. There is another lady in town named Marla who is a long-time friend of Brenda. Though I am only mentioning her now, she meets us at church and almost every sporting event. Her son, Matthew, is the same age as our boys and just another goofball to add to the list. That said Matthew and James are the two most mature of the bunch.

Brenda, Marla, and Lisa quickly adopt the name YaYa Sisters. The three of them are inseparable. We have kid stories, YaYa stories, Mark and Bruce stories. Every day is a challenge to see who is going to have the best day. I am struggling to remember my last bad day. Life is good. I remember the day that the YaYa sisters bought baseball jerseys with names on the back that associated with Abbott and Costello's skit *Who's On First*.

Well, it's the end of May 2007 and school is about to let out for the summer. That means it's time for another Report Card Day. So, Mr. 007 whose name was changed to 50/50 now has all A's and B's with one D. He is passing all his classes. This is amazing! Bruce's boys are all good. Let's eat! Time to go to Tapa!

Now that we have a lady (Lisa) visiting the house a few things must change. So, we got a second refrigerator and added one more rule to the Dude Ranch. The old refrigerator will be used for the boys and the new refrigerator will be for the adults. You are not going to believe this. In all the years following, that rule was never broken.

It is impossible to exaggerate the influence Lisa has on Travis, even now. Lisa, like Brenda, has this way about her that makes you genuinely not want to disappoint her. It was amazing to watch. I used conflict and confrontation tools for parenting Travis. Lisa used shame; she can make you feel bad for disappointing her and her method works. It even works on me!

It's summer 2007. Lisa is a high school teacher, and we are blessed that she can hangout at 715 and keep the boys from destroying the place. The boys are doing summer workout to prepare for the upcoming football season. This will be Travis's first year playing high school football. Remember those weights we bought at Academy? Well, they are in his room and evidently Travis, who is built like a fat stick figure, uses them. He has gained about 20-25 pounds. He is a good boy. He has love all around him. He is learning about love and family, just like me.

It's June 2007 and the second year goes by at the office without a pay increase. I love the job, it's another extended family, and I'm still working 50-60 hours a week. I'm almost finished automating our financials. Automating means that once the accounting department has completed their work for the previous month then you simply click a button and all the financials for that month as well as year-to-date are printed in the correct format, etc. What used to take a couple months is now done within a few minutes. This was a difficult task and badly needed.

It's early September 2007 and Lisa and I are getting married next month on October 26th.

Christian Hebrew Study

It's June 2022 and Sunday School is a privilege. It's wonderful to have an outlet to share what you have learned. I work from home and get my job done. It's demanding. Then I voluntarily spend long hours of research and preparation for class. I am spending a lot of time in the Lazy Boy recliner and one of my students told me I am starting to look pregnant. I know, gee thanks, right? Well, it's true, I am not sleeping much, and life is sedentary.

There were three or four adults in the class that learned the Hebrew letters. One of them even wrote a really cool program that you can use on your phone to help learn the letters. Isn't that cool? There doesn't seem to be any outspoken negativity about including the depth of understanding provided by including the Hebrew translations of the nouns of common stories.

The pastor of the church advised me that a group of men are teaming up to partner in building a chicken coop at each other's place and asked if I would be interested in joining the group. They included me, that's awesome! I accepted. Later, I learned that he had already received his chicks and they were in his garage, so this schedule needs to begin.

The following day pastor gave me a ride to one of the guys in this group that already had a chicken coop. This guy had a *cute* chicken coop, it was painted white and blue. I didn't say anything, but I am incapable of duplicating this chicken coop.

It seemed like a couple weeks later and still no evidence that the "5-man" chicken coop effort is going to materialize. Then Lisa shows me a Facebook picture of the pastor and his daughter loading wood at the local lumber store. Upon review of the picture, it is obvious he has never done this. I called him and he gave me more details of what he wanted to build, and we agreed to meet the following day. I worked all night and designed the entire chicken coop including a bill of materials. I created a video of the project and posted it on YouTube then sent him a text with the video link the following morning. He was blown away and proudly forwarded the link to our common friends.

The following morning, I hooked up my double-axle trailer and we loaded the wood he purchased and returned it. They credited his credit card. We then loaded all the material listed on the bill of material from the design I made the previous night. It took three carts of materials as we headed to checkout.

While waiting at checkout the wife of the man that built the white and blue chicken coop sees us in line. What are the odds, right? Her and the pastor share small talk. She and her husband are very nice people. She saw that we have a lot of materials and asked what we were building. When we told her we were building a chicken coop, she shared her story about how her husband built theirs. I remember it was a story I could never compare. She meant well but ouch! I digress. The pastor does not know me, nor my building standards and her husband has credibility, I don't. But I'm here and already this job is becoming an act of love. It just feels good.

The clerk rings up the materials and I quickly handed her my credit card and paid for everything. He was surprised and I only replied to him to allow me to be a blessing. My other motive is that I didn't want to be a disappointment so if I pay for everything then nobody gets to complain about my building designs. I am a mechanical engineer that has been friends with Bruce for over fifteen years. Bruce is a master carpenter, and I learned a lot about building standards during our visits. Besides that, I know me. I know what it takes to be my friend or to even be in my presence. I am high strung and getting older didn't fix it.

We begin the work and within a couple days we hear that the blue and white chicken coop experienced a break-in by racoons and all their chickens were gone. Ouch! That hurts. Pastor still doesn't know me and if I were him, I would be a little concerned about whether I knew what I was doing. That said, I'm not sure why, but with humor he shares the racoon break-in news with my sweet Lisa, and she replies, "Don't worry about that, Mark builds Ft. Knox." My Lisa is the best *wifey* on the planet. We made many jokes about us now building Ft. Knox.

The job continues and it was a great experience. We had such a great time working together, or at least that's my story. With humor, he kept pointing out the evidence of lack of engineering. Then I would explain that I got my engineering degree from Louisiana, not MIT. Another time, he starts playing Cajun music. Just saying, we had a great time.

The job is done. Yes Lisa, it's Ft. Knox. The entry door had a custom hinge, and I demonstrated its strength by hanging on it while he would swing it open and closed. It didn't sag a fraction. Pastor tried to make a love offering but no way was I accepting that. This is going into my eternal diary of love. This was a once in a lifetime experience. Thank you, Lord!

More Christian Hebrew Study

It's September 2022 and the church has disassociated from the United Methodist organization. We are now an independent church and have a new organization chart with four elders. I was asked and accepted the position as Deacon of Education. Sunday School is wonderful, attendance is back to normal and because we have a lack of volunteer teachers, I am also sharing duties teaching children's church during service. It is a privilege to serve but truly disappointed that I am incapable of influencing others to participate as a Sunday School teacher. It has also been decided to merge two of the adult Sunday School classes next month.

Honor of Kings

My condensed retelling of the traditional passed down story of Jonah is that he fled from God in rebellion and boarded a boat headed for Tarshish. He was then found to be the cause of bad weather threatening the lives of the crew and was rightfully thrown overboard. He was swallowed by a great fish where he resided for three days while being taken through the depths and then vomited onto shore. He then preached at Nineveh, and everyone repented and was then covered by what the KJV calls a gourd. Ok, I am quite aware that this condensed version leaves out a lot of amazing understanding but even after adding all the details to the passed down version, it's still the familiar Jonah story. Much like the earlier retelling of Samson, my Hebrew research revealed a *far* different story than the passed down traditions. My continued research has added to my understanding of this story as well as corrected my past teaching.

Earlier it was mentioned that the name Jonah translated to English is Dove. It is commonly known that the dove is a symbol of the Holy Spirit. Let's take that understanding to an extreme in the story of Jonah and then prove that the extreme is true. Let's temporarily rename the Book of Jonah as the Book of the Holy Spirit and then expect everything that we know about the Holy Spirit to be revealed.

We will begin this revelation by skipping the part of the story where Jonah fled from God, but we will come back to it. We know that the phrase "fled from God" doesn't play well as a character of the Holy Spirit so obviously there is something we must learn before we can make sense of it. That said, the first exercise to reveal that this is the Book of the Holy Spirit is by comparing the story of Jonah with the story of Jesus. The Book of Jonah and the Gospels of Jesus share a common story about an experience on a boat as well as what appears to be some resemblance of a resurrection. Let's review and compare these "boat stories" with the expectation of revealing (Gilgal) the concealed Holy Spirit in the Book of Jonah.

Let's give the boat story in the Book of Jonah the name "Jonah's boat" and likewise we will call the story in the Gospels "Jesus's boat".

The first thing to determine is where Jonah is from. We know that Jesus is a Galilean from Nazareth. In 2 Kings 14:25 we learn that Jonah, son of Amittai, is from Gath-Hepher which is a small town about five miles south of Nazareth. Jonah is Galilean as well.

- Jonah is Galilean.
  - Jesus is Galilean.

Ok, so 2 Kings 14:25 also tells us that Jonah's father's name is Amittai and it translates to English as My Truth.

- Jonah is Galilean.
  - Jesus is Galilean.
- Jonah's father is My Truth
  - Jesus's father is Yahweh. I'm okay with calling him My Truth in this story. Agree?

John 7:52 KJV: They answered and said unto him, Art thou also of Galilee? Search, and look: for out of Galilee ariseth no prophet.

In John 7:52 a Pharisee claims that Jesus is not a prophet because he is unaware that a prophet ever came from Galilee. Both Jesus and Jonah are declared not to be prophets within the same verse. .

- Jonah is Galilean.
  - Jesus is Galilean.
- Jonah's father is My Truth
  - Jesus's father is Yahweh. I'm okay with calling him My Truth in this story. Agree?
- Didn't believe Jonah was a prophet (John 7:52)
  - Didn't believe in Jesus was a prophet.

Jonah gets on his boat in Joppa and is headed to Tarshish. Joppa in Hebrew means beautiful and Tarshish in Hebrew means "yellow jasper". Hmm, I have a problem. If I do an internet search (which is subject to change from day-to-day) for "Tarshish Hebrew name meaning" it tells me "Yellow Jasper".

The Hebrew word for Tarshish is תרשיש and is in the original Hebrew twenty five times and is always translated as either Tarshish or Topaz. This is very significant because now we are going to reference these stones with those on the breastplate of the High Priest to determine if the tribe associated with the stone reveals further understanding.

The jasper stone is the last stone on the 4th row of the High Priest Breastplate and represents the tribe of Benjamin whose name means "Son of My Right Hand". I wish that was the right stone, it would make this story a slam dunk, right? If that were correct, then the Holy Spirit is getting on a boat headed from Beautiful to The Son of My Right Hand. I love it, I want to tell that story! We will see that there is a list of reasons why that's not the right story. Most Biblical translations would lead you down the path of the Jasper Stone, and you would reach a dead end trying to explain why Jonah was hurled into the sea and never reached The Son of My Right Hand.

The topaz stone is the middle stone on the first row of the breastplate and represents the tribe of Simeon whose name means "Hearing". Oh my, this is PERFECT! Let me explain.

The significance of **hearing** is a character trait described consistently throughout the Bible and is almost always concealed. The most common way that it is concealed is through the role of the name Simeon as well as the tribe of Simeon throughout the Bible. The Bible is loaded with concealed references of hearing.

- Joseph kept Simeon (hearing) in prison until the brothers returned with Benjamin (the son of my right hand).
- Moses blessed the tribes of Israel, but he did not bless Simeon (hearing). He knew that Israel would not hear, and the gentiles would.
- Jesus said, "those who have ears, let them hear."
- The Holy Spirit gets on a boat and is headed to Hearing.
- Jesus is brought to the temple on the 8th day and is circumcised by a man named Simeon (hearing). Coincidence? (Luke 2:25-26)

Luke 2:25-26 KJV: 25 And, behold, there was a man in Jerusalem, whose name was *Simeon*; and the same man was just and devout, waiting for the consolation of Israel: and the Holy Ghost was upon him. 26 And it was revealed unto him by the Holy Ghost, that he should not see death, before he had seen the Lord's Christ.

Jesus departed Capernaum and in Matthew 8:18 it tells us He simply headed to the other side. Capernaum means Village of Nahum. Village in Hebrew means to cover or protect, and Nahum in Hebrew means Comforter. Yes, the book of Nahum translated to English is the Book of the Comforter. Oh my, this is crazy amazing, right? So, Jesus is departing the Covering of the Comforter to go to the other side.

- Jonah is Galilean.
    - Jesus is Galilean.
- Jonah's father is My Truth
    - Jesus's father is Yahweh. (a.k.a. My Truth?)
- Didn't believe Jonah was a prophet (John 7:52)
    - Didn't believe in Jesus was a prophet.
- Jonah's boat is departing Beautiful and headed to Hearing.
    - Jesus's boat is departing the Covering of the Comforter to go to the other side.

In Jonah 1:3 it tells us that Jonah paid a fare before getting on the boat, but we know that Jesus did not. We will document and search this out while continuing the story.

- Jonah is Galilean.
    - Jesus is Galilean.
- Jonah's father is My Truth
    - Jesus's father is Yahweh. (a.k.a. My Truth?)
- Didn't believe Jonah was a prophet (John 7:52)
    - Didn't believe in Jesus was a prophet.
- Jonah's boat is departing Beautiful and headed to Hearing.
    - Jesus's boat is departing the Covering of the Comforter to go to the other side.
- Jonah pays a fare.
    - Jesus does not pay a fare.

In both stories they go to the bottom of the boat and sleep.

- Jonah is Galilean.
    - Jesus is Galilean.
- Jonah's father is My Truth
    - Jesus's father is Yahweh. (a.k.a. My Truth?)
- Didn't believe Jonah was a prophet (John 7:52)
    - Didn't believe in Jesus was a prophet.
- Jonah's boat is departing Beautiful and headed to Hearing.
    - Jesus's boat is departing the Covering of the Comforter to go to the other side.

- Jonah pays a fare.
  - Jesus does not pay a fare.
- Jonah goes to sleep at the bottom of the boat.
  - Jesus goes to sleep at the bottom of the boat.

Let's review the passengers on the boats. Jonah's boat has gentile unbelievers. Jesus's boat has His Disciples, Jewish believers.

- Jonah is Galilean.
  - Jesus is Galilean.
- Jonah's father is My Truth
  - Jesus's father is Yahweh. (a.k.a. My Truth?)
- Didn't believe Jonah was a prophet (John 7:52)
  - Didn't believe in Jesus was a prophet.
- Jonah's boat is departing Beautiful and headed to Hearing.
  - Jesus's boat is departing the Covering of the Comforter to go to the other side.
- Jonah pays a fare.
  - Jesus does not pay a fare.
- Jonah goes to sleep at the bottom of the boat.
  - Jesus goes to sleep at the bottom of the boat.
- Jonah's boat has gentile unbelievers.
  - Jesus's boat has disciples, Jewish believers.

This is where it gets interesting. It would seem as though the two stories take different paths. In Jonah 1:4 God sends a great wind into the sea and the ship was like to be broken, not filled with water. Note that it doesn't say there was a storm, it's a wind, a great wind sent by God. Consider that on the Day of Pentecost there was a sound like a rushing mighty wind. Just saying. Let's see what happens next on Jesus's boat.

In Luke 8:23 we learn that there came down a storm of wind. Hmm, is came down a storm of wind the same as a great wind sent by God? I vote yes. In Acts 2:2 it tells us that on the Day of Pentecost that "suddenly there came a sound from heaven as of a rushing mighty wind". Is there any chance that the wind came from the same place for these two boats? So, Jonah's boat with gentiles is experiencing wind from God as it about to break while Jesus's boat is experiencing wind and taking on water (apparently from waves) and is about to sink. The unbeliever's boat is breaking while the believer's boat is taking on water.

- Jonah is Galilean.
    - Jesus is Galilean.
- Jonah's father is My Truth
    - Jesus's father is Yahweh. (a.k.a. My Truth?)
- Didn't believe Jonah was a prophet (John 7:52)
    - Didn't believe in Jesus was a prophet.
- Jonah's boat is departing Beautiful and headed to Hearing.
    - Jesus's boat is departing the Covering of the Comforter to go to the other side.
- Jonah pays a fare.
    - Jesus does not pay a fare.
- Jonah goes to sleep at the bottom of the boat.
    - Jesus goes to sleep at the bottom of the boat.
- Jonah's boat has gentile unbelievers.
    - Jesus's boat has disciples, Jewish believers.
- Jonah's boat experiencing wind from God and about to break.
    - Jesus's boat experiences wind (from God?) and is about to sink.

Now we have an amazing profound divergence between these two stories. At this moment the men on both boats are fearing their lives and each is going to approach Jonah or Jesus to save them. Let's see the divergence of how the unbeliever and the believer are saved.

On Jonah's boat they are doing everything possible to save themselves. They throw everything overboard to lighten the load. Is it fair to say that the fare Jonah paid was thrown overboard? Hmm, how do we apply that? The Hebrew word for Fare (שכרה) in Jonah 1:3 is only used one time in scripture. Upon research you will also find this to be the only time in the translations that "a fare" is paid. Note that an offering or a tithe are not the same as paying a fare. Don't you love it when Hebrew and the English translation agree? The definition of the Hebrew letters for this word (שכרה) is, "The destruction (ש) of the hand that holds (כ) the prince (ר) will be revealed (ה)". Furthermore, if you remove the last letter that says it will be revealed then you have the phrase, "The destruction (ש) of the hand that holds (כ) the prince (ר)" which is in the Hebrew text 29 times and refers to being irritated or irritated due to intoxicant. Bottom line is that it appeared to have grieved the spirit to be required to pay a fare.

Next, gentile passengers on Jonah's boat are praying to their gods. Notice that they are not bailing water. Their boat isn't sinking, it's breaking. Finally, after nothing works, they awaken Jonah and ask him how he can sleep at such a time, and they request that Jonah do what they are doing and pray to his god.

On Jesus's boat, there isn't any hint in the story that the men did anything. There is no hint of prayer, likewise they awaken Jesus and simply asks him to save them.

Believers know where to find salvation, unbelievers need help to learn where to find salvation.

- Jonah's boat - the unbelievers do everything they can before awakening Jonah and asking him to join them in the effort to save them. They don't ask Jonah to save them, they simply ask for his help.
    - Jesus's boat - the believers awaken Jesus and ask for him to save them.

We know that the last bullet point of these two stories is that the men on both boats will be saved but now we get to see beautiful understanding of salvation for unbelievers (gentiles) and believers (Jews).

On Jonah's boat the unbelievers had no idea that after Jonah was awakened that he would tell them what they must do to be saved. The first thing they did was cast lots to see which of them was the cause of this windstorm. These men are aware that this is an act of God, and it seems clear that Jonah is participating in this effort of casting lots. Wait, these are gentiles, and they are casting lots.

After casting lots they learn that this is the Holy Spirit's fault and they ask him four questions 1) his occupation, 2) where he was from, 3) what country he was from, 4) what people he is. The next several verses aren't easily condensed but when it is all said, they knew that they had to "lift up" Jonah and hurl him into the sea to be saved. It seems that they had already thrown everything overboard which is symbolic to separating themselves from the things of this world. They struggled with the requirement, but immediately after the gentiles lifted up Jonah and hurled him into the sea, the winds stopped, and they feared the Lord exceedingly, offered a sacrifice, and made vows. After hurling Jonah to his death, they repented and became believers of Jonah's God.

Jonah's boat story is contained in the first chapter of Jonah. Yes, there is crazy more that we will share about the Book of the Holy Spirit as we continue our book series *It's the Same Story Again*. Oh, here is a "15 second" bonus. The Hebrew root word for fish in Jonah 1:17 is spelled (דג) and this is the only time that the root word for fish is used in the Hebrew text. The definition of the word is, "The door of wealth" or "The door of the spirit". To be continued. Glory to the King!

I cannot hold back. I love what happens next on Jesus's boat. Remember, this is a boat of believers. First, the beginning of Luke Chapter 8 makes it clear that all twelve disciples are with him, so they are likely all twelve on the boat. I would like to share my conjecture of how this played out and then we will return to only acknowledging what scripture says.

My conjecture of what happens: Several of these men are accustomed to the weather changes on the Sea of Galilee but like Jonah's boat this wind is like none before. I struggle believing the men that know the sea, the fishermen, sat there while the boat was taking on water and did nothing. I believe that at least in the beginning they exercised their experience of what to do and when they saw it was a lost cause they awakened Jesus. Scripture describes their amazement when they witness the miracle, proof they didn't wake him up to knowingly perform this miracle. They had no idea that Jesus possessed authority over the wind. I enjoy retelling this story to friends and suggesting the idea that when they awakened him, they were holding a bucket to help bale water, their only answer to the problem. Play it out the way you like, but from the time the wind started to the moment they feared death, I don't think they just sat there. It also seems apparent that they didn't pray.

They awaken Jesus and He rebuked the wind and the raging water. Then in Luke 8:25 Jesus asks them, "Where is your faith?" Prior to getting on the boat, Jesus shared the parable of the Sower and the seed. They are with Jesus, and they are "hearing". Oh wait, after the unbelievers hurled Jonah off the boat, they continued their journey to Tarshish which means "hearing". Everybody is hearing!

Glory to the King!

Chapter 17

Bereshet (בראשית) - In The Beginning
The First Word from the mouth of God

Life

I can only estimate that it's September 2007 and with great joy I declare that I learned my first Hebrew word during a church service. I recall that everyone left church that day changed. Once again, Bruce, my brother from another mother, and I always took our family and extended family to lunch after church. Currently that is only about 15 people. We talked for an hour about how much the sermon on this Hebrew word Bereshet impacted our understanding of scripture.

We were at the table talking about our first Hebrew word. Neither of us had ever learned, Bereshet (בראשית). This is the first Word that our Creator ever spoke. The preacher simply put the word on the huge church screen and explained Hebrew just as I have been explaining. My local church actually preached on a Hebrew word, and I remember well that the preacher did an awesome job. Let's review the beautiful story told by the modern Hebrew letters that spell the word along with the paleo Hebrew pictograph.

Bereshet בראשית

Once again, Hebrew is read from right to left.

The first letter of the word is the Bet (ב) which means house. You can also see that the first paleo pictograph is a rectangle with what resembles an open door and hall to a house.

The second letter is Resh(ר) which means Prince or Head and you can see that paleo Hebrew pictograph is a head with what appears to be a crown. If you combine the first two letters you get the word Bar (בר). So, the head of the house is the Son.

The third letter is Alef (א) which is the first letter of the Hebrew alphabet and it's referred to as the God letter and its paleo symbol is the Ox Head. The first three letters combined spell the word Bara (ברא) which means created. So, the first two letters spell "Son" then the third spells "God" and the first three letters spell "Created". So, this confirms scripture that tells us, "The Son of God Created".

The fourth letter is the Shin (ש) which is destruction, and its paleo picture is teeth like grinding food. The first four letters (בראש) denote "the head of" or "the beginning of". So, the first four letters tell us the story "The Son of God who Created will be Destroyed from the Beginning".

The fifth letter is the Yod (י) which is the hand that does mighty deeds. Note that the paleo Hebrew pictograph reveals that the Hand starts from the Shoulder. The Hebrew word for Shoulder is Shechem, the name of a familiar town in the Bible. So, the first five letters (בראשי) tell us "The Son of God Created will be Destroyed By His Own Hand That Does Mighty Deeds from the Beginning.

The sixth letter is the Tav (ת) and it means Covenant and its paleo symbol is the cross which is similar to each person of a covenant making their mark. The letter Tav is the last letter of the Hebrew alphabet. So, the six letters that spell the word Bereshet (בראשית) tell us "The Son of God who Created all things will be Destroyed by His Own Hand That Does Might Deeds to Make a Covenant.

The English translation of the word Bereshet is "In The Beginning". What is also revealing is that when the letter Bet is added to a noun to form a new word it is translated as "In". So, the remaining five letters of the word Bereshet form Reshet (ראשית) which translated means "First Fruits". So Bereshet could also be translated as "In First Fruits". Well, we know that Jesus is the First Fruits from the grave which is called "The Resurrection". So Bereshet translated as "In the beginning" is also "In the Resurrection". "In the Resurrection" was the first words God ever spoke.

Preacher knocked it out of the park.

More Life

It's September 2007 and high school football has cranked up! It's Friday Night Lights in Texas. Our kids are sophomores and play JV football on the varsity field on Thursday nights. James, Jacob, Link, Hazelnut, Travis, and Matthew are playing, and we are pumped. It's so awesome hearing their names on the intercom. It's even more fun listening to the teenage rhetoric after the game.

Lisa is still teaching at Austin High School located on the other side of town about 45 minutes away. She can't make Thursday's but shows up on Friday nights.

Lisa and I have decided to get married in Gatlinburg, Tennessee, during the Fall changing of the leaves. I have visited Gatlinburg many times in my past, and I have a plan that will blow her mind for our honeymoon. A story she will never forget.

Christian Hebrew Study

It's October 2022 and the adult Sunday School classes merged and though everyone knows each other, three of my friends including the pastor are now elders and attending my class. The class went well but I could discern that the Hebrew insights included in my lesson weren't accepted well.

Honor of Kings

The original Hebrew holds amazing revelation about the name of God, Yahweh (יהוה). The word Yahweh (יהוה) is in the Hebrew Old Testament 6,007 times. The Hebrew word Elohim (אלהים) is in Hebrew scriptures 680 times and is also translated as God or Lord, including in Genesis 1:1.

The definition of the Hebrew letters that spell Yahweh is,

"The Hand(י) Reveals(ה), the Nail(ו) Reveals (ה)"

Is there an undisputable link between His name and Jesus on the cross? I remember when I was a very young, maybe 10 or 12 years old, watching the movie "The Greatest Story Ever Told". I remember the scene where they hung the sign over his head. I wasn't aware that it was in three languages. The sign read "Jesus the Nazarene King of the Jews". Only the Gospel of John provides any evidence that there was contention between the chief priest trying to get the wording of the sign changed. Both the scriptures and the movie draw your attention away from what is hidden in the Hebrew letters of that sign and bring your focus only to what the sign says. Below is that sign in Hebrew.

ישוע הנצרי ומלך היהודים

Do you see it? God (יהוה) conceals his glory in many ways within the original Hebrew words and letters. One of those is hiding a word within the first letters of words within a phrase. Let's look at the words of the sign again and as

you can see, I have emphasized what the chief priest saw that created the
contention in the Gospel of John.

יֵשׁוּעַ הַנֹּצְרִי וַמֶלֶך הַיְּהוּדִים

Now it is more obvious. Yet another instance where Jesus, his Hebrew
name being Yeshua's (ישוע) and the first word of the sign, is identified and
revealed for everyone that looked upon Him. The sign reads "Yeshua King of
the Jews". The Father, who never forsakes His Son, has his name concealed
within the first Hebrew letter of each word of the sign above Jesus's head. This
form of concealing understanding is commonly known within the Hebrew
community. I am convinced that the chief priests were not offended by Jesus
being called "King of the Jews" but rather they didn't want the name Yahweh
(יהוה) revealed on the cross.

Chapter 18

Yeshua (ישוע) - The Hebrew name of Jesus

Life

It's October 25, 2007, and Lisa and I are boarding a plane to Knoxville, Tennessee, to get married the following day. I'm older now, I am supposed to be wiser, more loving, unselfish, and all the other character traits a man should embrace as he gets older. I have an amazing week planned for my sweet Lisa.

I am convinced that this plan only works with someone like Lisa. I know her, she is incapable of telling a lie or even misrepresenting herself. My plan would exercise that character trait.

After we get into our seat on the airplane I told Lisa, "Ok, here is the deal, any time this week that you get bored, just tell me." She agreed and the plane takes off while we visit. I am not amazed that she hasn't told me she is bored. Finally, after about 30 minutes I ask her, "Are you bored?"

She replies, "Yes."

I then reach in my sports jacket and hand her a 3"x5" greeting card that has #1 written on the front. She opens the greeting card, and the personalized message tells her that we are flying to Knoxville to get married and a few more comments about this special moment. What's key is that the card accurately identifies where we are. It was a calculation on my part, but I just knew she wouldn't say she was bored twice while on the plane. And she didn't. I have many of these cards prewritten for the events I have prescheduled for the week. Enjoy the story as it plays out.

We arrived at Knoxville and are now driving the rental car to Gatlinburg. We are trying to find the office of the travel agency so that we can get the key and address of our cabin rental. I know, what's the big deal, right? No, I won't include details of every time we stop at a red light! The big deal is that it's dark and the address of the travel agency can't be found. Then Lisa says, "Let's go to that shopping center over there." So, I pull in and she says, "Go look in that box and see if our reservations are in it?"

Ok, that just sounds too easy to be true, right? There is no way to exaggerate what just happened. The address is not the one provided on the travel agency's itinerary. There isn't a sign with the travel agency's name anywhere and I open this publicly accessible box located on the side of this business in this shopping center and there is an envelope with my name on it. I can't explain it but the day is saved, and we go to our cabin.

The next morning, we are getting ready for our wedding and realize that we do not have a marriage license. That's what happens when you get married at an old age. That stuff just doesn't matter until the moment that it does. Luckily, it's a Friday and we were able to acquire the license. Yay! Only hours before the wedding! Most people would freak out. Lisa and I were prepared to sign a napkin if needed. There was literally zero stress, and we are now headed to breakfast.

Lisa saw me walking into the restaurant with a large greeting card. After we sat down, I handed her the card. I preplanned where we would eat each meal. I knew it would mess up the surprise if I told her and she never asked. She liked me being her personal tour guide and picking all the restaurants. That's why this was doable. She opens the card knowing that it was written prior to this morning because we had been together, and she would have seen me writing it. She is finally impressed that the card includes the place where we are sitting and that it's breakfast time before our wedding and more lovely words. She still hasn't figured out the role of these greeting cards.

Our wedding was at a retired chaplain's residence. Pastor Rob was amazing at making private moments special. We only had a couple squirrels witness our wedding. After we said our vows, he took us near wind chimes and made it chime then told Lisa, "Every time you hear wind chimes you guys must kiss." At the time I am writing, we have been married more than 16 years and to this day we kiss every time we hear wind chimes regardless of where we are. Thank you, Pastor Rob.

We are married and it's time for lunch. You guessed it. Here is your card and once again she is only slightly impressed and still does not realize this is going to be a routine at every meal of the week. Nope, she still hasn't asked me for the second "I'm Bored" card. Surely, you are amazed, right? Any other person would have said they were bored five times while on the plane. Lisa didn't say she was bored because she wasn't.

It's time to take my bride, my sweet Lisa, to Cade's Cove inside The Great Smoky Mountain National Park. It's the end of October and this is the busiest time of the year for tourists because the Fall leaves are changing colors. This is a two-week nature event and witnessing the change each day is spectacular. I would actually make jokes about a specific leaf on a specific tree that I realized had changed colors from the previous day. Lisa is laughing at my craziness. We are entering Cade's Cove and Lisa says, "Hey, I am bored."

I reach into my pocket and almost certain she sees that I have several cards and I hand her the "I Am Bored Card #2". She is finally stunned that the card states we are driving thru Cade's Cove and yet another unique message about why I love her. She now has evidence that these cards have been pre-written and are numbered on the cover of the envelope. Now it is fun. In my preparations I knew that once she figured this out that she would likely be more aware of her boredom. I planned on her asking more often. I planned on her enjoying a specific view of the park and saying she is bored to find out if the next card talked about the scene she is experiencing. Yes, I have been to the park more than ten times. Every year I try to witness the Fall color changes. This is an amazing place to be married and an amazing place to visit each year for your anniversary. This is perfect and Lisa's first-time visiting Gatlinburg.

It's the next day. The greeting card program has a perfect score and we have eaten breakfast and decided to stop at one of those tourists' places that dress you up in old country clothes of the past for a picture. Lisa is holding a replica shot gun to my neck and while the photographer is focusing, she told me, "If you ever leave me, I will shoot you."

The photographer can't ignore Lisa's beautiful spirit, the tone of her voice, nor the content of her words. It is quite apparent that the most beautiful woman on the planet has married a toad. He is trying to find the words to ask me a question and I interrupted him and said, "If you screw this up for me!" as we both laughed.

He said, "You are one lucky man."

Just before taking the picture, he told Lisa to give her mean face.

He changes our pose and gets ready to take the second picture and once again tells Lisa to give her mean face. He stops and looks at me and asks, "Am I wasting my time?"

I replied, "I don't understand, she's giving you her mean face." We are both laughing, and he is just another witness to my sweet Lisa.

The entire week was amazing. There is not a single second of discord, debate, confrontation, irritation, or anything less than unspeakable joy. It's our last day and we are going to have breakfast before returning to Knoxville. Our last meal card has the restaurant name included in the message. While driving to breakfast Lisa asked if she could pick the restaurant. Oh, oh, this is going to be interesting. There are two restaurants about a half-mile ahead so I have a 50/50 chance she will pick the one on the card. Bingo! She picked the correct restaurant. We went inside and laughed as she read her card.

As we left the restaurant, I realized that the car keys were not in my pocket. I return to our table, and they aren't there. After a bit of discussion to trace our steps Lisa says, "Let's just head back to the car and see if they show up." Sound familiar?

Yes, when we got to the grass median near where we were parked, I looked down and found our car keys. No kidding, the week ended like it started. Mark and Lisa Stroderd are returning to 715.

More Life

It's October 26, 2013, and we are headed to Gatlinburg to celebrate our wedding anniversary. There is a special story that takes place on this visit unlike any of our past. On our first night we went to a restaurant for dinner. It's cold and we are wearing our Texas A&M hoodies. The folks at the table behind Lisa are wearing NFL Cleveland Browns attire. I have made many business trips to Cleveland in my past. It was a privilege to experience the completion of the Cleveland Flats project. That's a story to be told.

After a few minutes one of the men at that table asked me if I thought Johnny Manziel was going to be a good quarterback for the Browns. If you are unaware, Johnny won the NCAA Football Heisman Trophy the previous year and was drafted by the Cleveland Browns. I loved this guy's spirit, and we had a great conversation where I convinced him that was yet another of a long line of Cleveland mistakes. There were two couples at the table and the wives were getting an unscheduled ESPN update on the subject. While we were talking, two couples wearing Pittsburgh Steelers attire walked into the restaurant. Hilarious, I knew the culture of Browns fans and it was no surprise when this guy says, "I hate Steeler fans. No, I mean it. When I see them, I just want to go punch them in the face."

Lisa is shocked but it was so funny to be able to talk to this guy with a kindred spirit because it was obvious that I was familiar with Cleveland fans. We all had a great laugh. Oh, one more thing, those two men got to hear Lisa talk to their wives for a couple minutes. Yes, I have a secret weapon for handling bad spirits. All I do is let Lisa answer a question. Usually within a couple minutes EVERYBODY LOVES LISA, and the tigers are tame, and the angels start singing kumbaya. (laughing)

The next day Lisa and I were making our traditional anniversary walk in downtown Gatlinburg and there they were. These same two couples, the Browns fans, were sitting in lounge chairs in front of their hotel. We chatted a bit and it was fun.

That night Lisa and I attended one of the live shows in Pigeon Forge. It was common to take the traditional overpriced tourist picture in the lobby of the show. After taking the picture we went inside to be seated and we heard people calling our names. There they were. This is the 3rd time in two days that we have *bumped* into these guys. I told Lisa to go buy their souvenir pictures during intermission and bring it to them. I know, that's mean, right? I've decided that meeting them three times in two days couldn't possibly be a coincidence. My Savior is always busy with his work. All I must do is drive Ms. Daisy and watch it happen. (laughing) Ms. Daisy still has no clue that she is Ms. Daisy, that's why she is still Ms. Daisy.

Yep, you guessed it, our last day before heading back and there they are on the opposite side of the street. They are yelling so we cross over to visit. The two men asked if they could visit me privately while Lisa chats with their wives. We step around the side of a building and these two men begin crying. They are telling me how wonderful me and Lisa are and how they are going back home and making honest women out of these two ladies that they have put off marrying. They keep talking and share that they are never going to let football have a hatred spirit with their lives and they just keep talking until they finally asked me to pray for them. We prayed and we all went our own way, and nobody exchanged phone numbers or emails. It's just another day with Lisa in Gatlinburg.

Christian Hebrew Study

It's Sunday, October 16, 2022, and last week I could feel some tension after the first week adult classes were merged. Again, my friends who are also elders of the church are in class. As mentioned at the end of class last week, today I am teaching on the circle(s) of life as they are related to the letters of the Hebrew Alphabet, our Father's language. Remember me? I am "That Guy" that is constantly working to wear out his welcome.

You are about to learn the origin of why this section of the story is named "Christian Hebrew Study". Church and Hebrew are not a friendly combination. Few can accept that Christians can learn Hebrew without embracing Judaism. To convert to Judaism means you cease believing in Jesus as your Savior. There isn't the slightest hint that I would do that. After learning Hebrew I found that to be ludicrous. I have not witnessed any of my Christian friends that know Hebrew deny the Salvation of the Gospel. Nonetheless, not to understand that's how people think and constantly guarding against this misunderstanding is an extreme lack of wisdom. You are also going to witness another blessed and miraculous moment in the lives of Mark and Lisa.

I am loving the privilege to teach the topic and when class is finished one of the attendees is telling me about how her father had the kids recite the Hebrew Shema every night before bed. Yes, her family is Christian, and they grew up quoting the Shema, "Hear, O Israel: YHWH is our God, YHWH is one". It would have been awesome if this most influential lady would have shared that in class. While she is sharing this, I notice my friends who are elders leaving class with an unpleasant countenance. This was the second weekend that adult classes were merged.

That night I got a phone call from one of the elders and he simply asked, "Mark, is the King James Bible the divine and inspired Word of God?" Well this book has effectively answered that question many times.

I answered my memorized reply when asked this question, "Today, the King James Bible is one of over one hundred English translations of the divine and inspired Word of God." There were a few seconds of words and we hung up.

The pastor asked me to meet him at his home around noon on Thursday to inspect his beehives. Prior to building his chicken coop, I participated in funding part of the cost to get him into the wonderful hobby of beekeeping. Lisa and I had been beekeepers for four years prior to moving to Medina.

After of couple hours of work and visiting the pastor, he expressed that he had to share some bad news. He told me, "Mark, you are one of the most intelligent people I have ever met. I just don't have a way to say this nicely, but before you showed up, we had an elders meeting and we voted unanimously to remove you from Deacon of Education at the church."

By now you know that I can connect dots very fast and without hesitation I replied, "Pastor you are breaking my heart. Are you okay if I find another church to attend?"

He replied, "Yes."

That was **_NOT_** the answer I wanted but I shook his hand and immediately left the property.

Before going any further, it is **_CRITICAL_** that you understand that it took me a while, but I finally realized this was **100% my fault**. So, while I share how I came to understanding, do not judge anyone that participated in this story. Don't judge me, pastor, or the elders. No, at the time of this book, the story isn't over, but the end of the story is visible. Lisa and I are blessed to witness God's healing.

I will skip the pain-filled days and move forward a year later to October 25, 2023. Guess where me and Lisa are? Yep, we are at Gatlinburg for our anniversary and watching the Fall color change. Yes, we were here last year, which was two weeks after the news. I am committed to not taking my kids or anyone else down a road of pain that could lead to bitterness without first showing that the pain was healed. After healing, clarity reveals itself.

This year's visit to Gatlinburg is different than any of our past. We have friends meeting us. Our friends Berk and Olga drove from Medina to witness the Fall color change for the first time. I also have long-time friends from the past coming to visit. I prefer not to mention their names so let's call them Bob and Sue. Bob and I attended the same church for five years from 1982-1987 while living in my hometown, Lake Charles, La. He is now a pastor of several campuses of churches he founded. He decided to make the trip after one of our many Bible study phone conversations where I share some of the revelations about Hebrew in this book. He is there for a personal Bible study that required us to be physically present.

We all arrived late the first night and now it is about noon the following day and we are sitting on the porch of Berk and Olga's cabin next to a rock bottom creek with a small amount of water flowing this time of the year. It's beyond beautiful.

I asked Bob and Sue if they were ready to have this lesson since they would be leaving the next day and there wouldn't be a better time or place to do so. Everyone agreed as I taught the lesson. Most of the lessons have already been shared so I won't repeat them, but it is worth sharing how the lessons began.

I asked Pastor Bob, "Can you explain the significance of both water and blood pouring from Jesus's body when they pierced Him on the cross?"

Bob didn't get defensive or try to explain, he just replied, "No."

We know each other well but Berk and Olga don't know Bob. I had to express, "That's why I love you, Bob. I believe very few Pastors know the answer to that, but they would either walk away when I ask the question or start defending why they don't know."

I asked Bob another question, "Bob, do you have an explanation for the people that Jesus told to depart from Him because He didn't know who they are?"

Sue, his wife chimed in, but I cut her off fairly quickly suggesting she is repeating passed-down church rhetoric that cannot be proven scripturally. Yes, these are my friends, and we love each other so we don't have to spend 30 minutes measuring our words to speak a sentence. Sue agreed.

Bob replied to the question, "Bro. Mark I do not have an answer for that story, and I have never met a preacher willing to discuss it. I distance myself from things in the Bible I cannot explain. This is one of them."

I then shared that I have one last question, "Who is Paul talking about in Romans 7:1 when he expresses, he is talking to those that know the law and what is so important for him to share that?"

Bob replies, "He is talking about the Jews, right?"

It was an amazing Bible study that I will share in detail in the next book of this series. What's key is to see that I never stopped researching the original Hebrew of His Word and Bob is proof that the only requirement to share "Christian Hebrew" study without the potential for judgment is that everyone participating loves each other. That was my mistake in my last Sunday School lesson. I am guilty as much as anyone in the room of not loving. I didn't love them enough to have previously empathized with how they would receive the lesson. I knew there was discord from the previous week, and I ignored it. I know where all the elders of the church live and all of them would have welcomed a visit. I am without excuse. There is more but the bottom line is they were not given the eight-month introduction that the rest of the class was privileged to hear. It's their second week in my class and they were exposed to one hour of teaching the Hebrew alphabet.

The elders had recently exhausted themselves disassociating from an organization that allows drag queens to be ministers. They are newly appointed to be accountable for the Church's doctrine and now they are hearing a one-hour lesson on the letters of Hebrew. I keep asking myself why I didn't start over from the beginning. Why didn't I reteach Ruth or Samson to reveal the beauty of Christian Hebrew and give them a chance to witness how Hebrew enhances what we know and that it is not whatever it is falsely perceived to be? WHAT WAS I THINKING? Great lesson, wrong time. Many of the lessons in this book would have been far more appropriate. The fourth chapter of this book, titled "Donkey", would have been an amazing study to introduce these guys to Christian Hebrew study. Anything other than a class about the Hebrew alphabet. Great passion, poor wisdom. My apologies to all!

The one-year story of events that began the day I was voted to be removed as Deacon of Education is heart-breaking. A story where I witnessed my sweet Lisa cry for many days. Our 2022 anniversary in Gatlinburg just two weeks following was our saddest moments ever spent in Gatlinburg. My apologies to my wife for missing the target on this. Thank you, Lisa, for being so gracious. Lisa and I are healed and there is a new beginning in Medina already revealing itself.

Looking forward to writing the next book in this series. We love the amazing people of our hometown, Medina, Tx. God bless all we love, all we have hurt, and all who have hurt us.

Glory to the King!

Honor of Kings

Wow, that is a hard story to follow, right? Well, as you can see, the Life section ended with our wedding in Gatlinburg in October 2007 and the Christian Hebrew Study section ended in Gatlinburg in October 2023. We have so much more to share about Bruce, Brenda, Lisa, the morons (smile), Life, and sadly a tragic accidental death within our group. But now, let's review this book's last effort of the Honor of Kings.

We have been searching out Hebrew nouns that were not translated into English. In the Jonah story we added another Book of the Bible to our list of nouns translated. The Name Nahum means Comforter. Check out the names of three books in the Bible that we have searched out the translation of their names.

- Book of Friend (Ruth)
- Book of Dove – "Book of The Holy Spirit" (Jonah)
- Book of The Comforter (Nahum)

Wouldn't it be awesome if there was a book named Jesus. Can you hear your preacher say, "Good morning, turn with me in your Bible to the Book of Jesus. We are reading in Chapter 7." I'm sure all of you can share a wise crack on that idea.

The last Hebrew word we will search out in Volume 1 is Yeshua (ישוע), Jesus's name in Hebrew. Is it possible to teach on The Name Above All Names and do it justice? I don't think so.

Before searching out the name Yeshua, let's first understand from where the name Jesus was derived. Jesus is *derived* from the Roman Catholic Latin[1] Iesus. The Roman Catholic Latin Iesus comes from the Ancient Greek[2] Ιεσους. The Ancient Greek Ιεσους is the Hellenized[3] version of the Aramaicized[4] Hebrew[5] name Yeshua. The English name Jesus is *derived* from five languages. Decide for yourself if *derived* implies it was translation or transliteration.

Jesus's Hebrew name is Yeshua. Yeshua translated into English is Salvation. Imagine substituting the word Salvation everywhere you see the word Jesus in scripture. Initially it would be very difficult but likely after repetitive reading it would become easier and likely even more understandable. Now, understand that the disciples and everyone in the Bible that knew Hebrew **new that they were calling Him by the name "Salvation"**.

Before continuing, let's once again review the sign that was placed above Yeshua while He was on the cross.

יֵשׁוּעַ הַנָּצְרִי וַמֶלֶךְ הַיְהוּדִים

This time Yeshua's name is in bold and larger font. The sign was translated earlier as "Yeshua King of the Jews". When His name is translated to English as we have done the other words, the sign reads "Salvation King of the Jews". Our Salvation was lifted up on a cross made from a Cedar Tree. Cedar means the Father (God א) and His Son (ר) are Perfect (ז). Tree means See (ע) Righteousness (צ). Our Salvation was lifted up on Cedar Tree cross that reveals the Father and the Son are Perfect and Righteous. Glory to the King!

Let's review the Hebrew letters that spell Yeshua. The first letter of Yeshua (ישוע) is the Hebrew letter Yod (י), and this letter represents the hand of God (יהוה) that does mighty deeds. As you can see, it is also the first letter of God's name, Yahweh. The second letter of Yeshua (ישוע) is the Shin (ש), and this letter represents destruction. The third letter of Yeshua (ישוע) is the Vav (ו), and this letter represents a straight-up man with a nail. The fourth and last letter of Yeshua (ישוע) is the Ayin (ע), and this letter represents an eye. My definition of the word Yeshua from the definition of the Hebrew letters is, "By His own hand that does mighty deeds (י) He was destroyed (ש) and is the straight-up man with the nail (ו) for everyone to see (ע). This is Salvation. This is a good time to restate the definition of His Father's name, Yahweh, "The Hand (י) Reveals (ה), the Nail (ו) Reveals (ה)". What a message!

Earlier we learned that the Resurrection story is concealed within the Old Testament Gilgal story. No surprise that story includes Joshua (יהושע - Yehoshua), which both sounds and is spelled very similar to Yeshua. In the teaching about Gilgal we learned how the Resurrection story is concealed in this story of Joshua taking God's people into the promised land. In Hebrew there are many words that translate to English as Salvation. The name Joshua and Hosea are two examples that we will search out later. That said, Salvation spelled with the exact spelling as Yeshua is only in the Hebrew scriptures nineteen times and only in the Book of Ezra (עזרא) whose name means Help and the Book of Nehemiah (נחמיה) whose name means God Comforts.

The original Hebrew text validates the Salvation of the Gospels. It does not provide an alternative Salvation. It does help to understand the Narrow Path that has been muddied by nearly two thousand years of the world's influence.

Glory to the King!